INFORMATION ANALYSIS
Second Edition

JOEL S. DEMSKI
Stanford University

INFORMATION ANALYSIS
Second Edition

ADDISON-WESLEY PUBLISHING COMPANY
Reading, Massachusetts • Menlo Park, California
London • Amsterdam • Don Mills, Ontario • Sydney

This book is in the
Addison-Wesley Paperback Series in Accounting

Consulting Editor
William J. Bruns, Jr.

Library of Congress Cataloging in Publication Data

Demski, Joel S
  Information analysis.

  (Paperback series in accounting)
  Bibliography: p.
  Includes index.
  1. Decision-making. 2. Management information
systems. I. Title.
HD30.23.D46   1980   658.4'038   80-15971
ISBN 0-201-01231-6 (pbk.)

ISBN 0-201-01231-6
ABCDEFGHIJ-DO-89876543210

To Millie

EDITOR'S FOREWORD

The environment for accounting has undergone revolutionary changes in the last decade. Demand for accountability by managers of both public and private organizations has risen significantly. Electronic data transmission, storage, and processing and other information technologies have developed to allow accountants to use methods and processes that would have been considered impossible, or uneconomical, just a few years ago. At the same time, new quantitative methods for solving accounting problems have been developed, and the behavioral sciences have suggested that the impact of accounting goes well beyond the systems and reports which are the most visible product of the accountant's work.

The speed with which these developments have occurred has made it difficult for teachers and students of accounting, and for managers and accountants themselves, to keep their knowledge up-to-date. New solutions to problems, and sometimes even new kinds of accounting problems themselves, are not treated in many textbooks. In addition, problems and solutions often cross boundaries between what were once considered separate disciplines of study. The student or manager seeking a learning aid in an era of change will frequently be frustrated. In many respects, materials which have been available do not reflect either the new developments or the unprecedented opportunities for creative thinking and problem solving which accounting presents.

Each book in this Addison-Wesley Series treats a new development or subject which has not been widely treated in textbooks which are widely available. In addition, because each book concentrates on a single set of problems, methods, or topics in accounting, each provides comprehensive coverage in an economical form. The Series was conceived to help all who work with or process accounting information, all of whom must continue to learn in order to keep pace with the changes which are occurring. Each book has been carefully developed by an outstanding scholar.

Books in this Series were prepared in the belief that the evaluation of accounting and its importance to managers will continue, and with faith that books are an effective means to assist all who are interested to participate in the developments which will take place in the future. Our goal has been to improve the practice and processes of accounting, and to help all who use accounting information to do so more effectively.

William J. Bruns, Jr.
Professor of Business
Administration
Harvard University

CONTENTS

PREFACE

This monograph is designed to provide the basis for a serious, but not exhaustive, study of the economic aspects of information. The typical accounting (or management information system) course makes extensive reference to the "cost and value of information." But exactly what such a phrase means, what its roots are, and how serious it is to be taken as a guide to action are typically not addressed. It is to this void that the monograph is addressed.

As such, this book is suitable for supplemental material in a managerial accounting course, second (or beyond) financial accounting course, second decision theory course, or management information systems course. It can also be used as the basis for a course that focuses on the economic aspects of information.

The monograph is quite distinct from its first edition predecessor. The original edition focused on information choice questions and on modeling considerations in capacity acquisition, short run output, and control decisions. Other than the general idea of a "cost effective" or simplified decision analysis, this latter material has been dropped from the second edition in favor of a more thorough analysis of information system questions. This reflects, in part, the growth in our understanding of the economic aspects of information. But it also reflects an attempt to keep the monograph conceptually balanced. While quite important, the question of designing or selecting cost effective models is subsumed by the question of selecting an information system. So at a sufficiently conceptual level, the material is covered as part of the information system question.

Prerequisites are always a difficult issue for supplementary material, and even more so with material that can be quite technical. You should be familiar with accounting to the extent that you are able to identify with the examples of and references to accounting questions. You should also have some grasp of decision theory, as would be produced in a typical business school curriculum. Otherwise, the continued use of expected utility analysis is likely to be disconcerting. Likewise, you should be able to solve two variable linear programming models simply because a few examples exploit the structure of linear programs. Nothing else is assumed, other than a taste for or tolerance of conceptual questioning. The monograph makes extensive use of the idea of a function and its more basic notion of a binary relation. These items are developed in Chapter 1. No other mathematical sophistication is entertained or relied upon.

Finally, Chapter 2 deals with measure theory and the axiomatic structure behind expected utility analysis. The chapter therefore stands out as being more conceptual or more "basic" than the others. As such, it need not be consumed prior to consumption of the remaining chapters. At the same time, however, you should recognize that your enjoyment of the remaining chapters will dramatically increase if you take the time and effort to work through the material in Chapter 2.

Numerous individuals have provided important factors in the production of this monograph. Jerry Feltham introduced me to the topic (years ago) and has continued to be a source of stimulation. David Ng and Mark Wolfson graciously critiqued an earlier draft of this edition. David Kreps is responsible for my learning the material developed in Chapter 6. Elena Lenz provided masterful typing. Finally, my wife, Millie, and my children have remained supportive during the entire process. To them I remain grateful and indebted.

Stanford, California   J. S. D.
May 1980

Chapter One

THE DIMENSIONS OF CHOICE

STAGES OF ANALYSIS
MATHEMATICAL PREREQUISITES
FOOTNOTES

The fundamental concern in this book is *information choice*. The basic premises are that (1) information is a commodity whose acquisition, like that of other commodities, constitutes a problem of economic choice, and (2) one can obtain insight into this vague problem by viewing information issues within the formal structure of the economics of uncertainty, or decision theory. Thus we shall approach the problem of information choice in a formal manner and concentrate on systematic analysis of information alternatives. This process of analysis will be termed *information analysis.*

Information analysis revolves around alternative methods of describing subsets of phenomena to some specific decision maker. Thus the basic element of choice is not the description itself; rather, it is the method of description and the set of phenomena described, where issues of time, form, content, and so on are all understood to be subsumed under the alternative methods. To illustrate, the accountant selects a method that will be used to estimate a firm's income over a recent period, but not the income number itself. We shall refer to such alternative methods of describing subsets of phenomena as alternative *information systems,* or more simply as alternative systems.

Each such system provides a (possibly random) set of descriptions to some specific decision maker. For example, using a particular method of estimating a firm's income results in a specific income number. Similarly, using a specific cost-variance reporting system results in a specific list of cost variances for some responsibility center for some reporting period. We refer to a specific set of descriptions as a *signal*. And since the signals are transmitted to a specific decision maker, we examine the information choice problem in a specific contextual setting.[1] The setting selected for expositional purposes is decision analysis in a firm. Other decision contexts could have been selected, but the firm's decisions emphasized here are among the more familiar and more formalized at this point in history. This provides, as we shall see, an important advantage.

Finally, we must also provide for the fact that the person who selects the system may not be—and likely will not be—the same person for whom the signals are intended. The firm's controller, for example, has a great deal to say about the accounting system, while others in the organization use the resulting signals in their decision making. We shall refer to the former as the *information evaluator* and to the latter as the *decision maker*. This raises a number of subtleties which combine with the topic's oblique nature to create an expositional problem. In an attempt to ease these difficulties, we shall approach the problem of analysis in four stages.

STAGES OF ANALYSIS

We begin with a serious look at assumptions. The study is largely based on the assumption that the evaluator engages in decision analysis of a choice problem; this manifests itself in the ubiquitous description of expected utility maximization. Since this is such an important assumption, we introduce the study in Chapter 2 by examining the assumptions that underly such a description of behavior.

Armed with expected utility maximization we then examine the case, in Chapter 3, in which the evaluator and the decision maker are the same person. The central theme here is that information analysis by the decision maker is a familiar subject to the student of decision theory. In particular, complete satisfaction of the assumptions of decision theory ensures that the impact of information is strictly limited to one of systematic probability revision. This enables us to treat the issue of information choice in a concise, formal way.

The third stage, Chapter 4, introduces the cost of the analysis implied by decision theory. This results in simplifications, or less than complete specification of the decision maker's problem. Uncertainty may be suppressed; the impacts of future periods may be ignored. Hopefully, the savings in analysis balance the opportunity cost of the resulting decision errors. Two significant implications emerge here. (1) Movement to a simplified model alters the potential impact of information from one of systematic probability revision to one of potential impact on any facet of decision activity. Many of these facets, due to simplifications, are not explicitly reflected in the decision model. Recognition of this fact leads us to conclude that the impact of additional information is particularly oblique in a simplified setting. (2) Alternative simplified models exist, and the question of which model to employ is itself a choice problem. Indeed, when we recognize that using a simplified model does not mean that the decision maker completely delegates a choice to the model, we see that the optimal solution obtained by using a simplified model provides the decision maker with information. Strictly speaking, then, the optimal decision indicated by the simplified model is *one,* but not necessarily *the,* determinant of the ultimate choice. Consequently, the issue of which simplified model to employ is merely a special case of the broader problem of which information system to use.

The fourth stage, Chapters 5 and 6, introduces a separate information evaluator. Specification of the decision maker's use of the information is important here. Chapter 5 treats this specification as given and examines the resulting analysis and anomalies in relation to the case where the evaluator and decision maker are not distinct. A limited amount of endogenous specification of the decision maker's behavior is explored in Chapter 6 where, after discarding the notion of group utility maximization, we focus on the structure of the decision maker's choice behavior being motivated by judicious design of an incentive system. Either way, the resulting information system choice will depend on the use made of the information by the decision maker. But knowledge of this use is not the sole determinant of the system choice. Thus the notion of a decision model's "information requirements" has no meaning in this analysis.

Finally, by way of summarization we briefly mention, in Chapter 7, possible extensions of our study to settings in which numerous decision makers trade in organized markets. The question of the information system itself being available in an "information market" is also briefly discussed.

MATHEMATICAL PREREQUISITES

Any study that proposes a "formal" or "rigorous" examination or that begins by looking at assumptions is a signal of possible mathematical difficulty for the student. But mathematical difficulty covers many sins; and it is important, therefore, to be precise about what the student is assumed to know. First the good news: no mathematical sophistication is required, entertained, or used in the succeeding chapters. (A single exception here is that the Calculus is used once to take partial derivatives of a quadratic equation in an example in Chapter 6.) Everything is based on finite *sets*. You are invited to explore the referenced literature, where the requisite sophistication becomes considerable at times.

Now for the bad news: the topic is treated in a formal way in the sense that assumptions are laid out and their implications are deduced and analyzed. Thus a taste, be it ever so slight, for the logical is assumed here.

To more directly advertise what is, and what is not, entailed in succeeding chapters, the use to be made of naive set theory should be made clear. Besides the usual and (presumed) familiar ideas of set membership, union, and intersection, two specific types of sets are emphasized: binary relations and functions.

To develop their meaning, consider the sets X and Y below:

$$X = \{a, \ b, \ c\}$$
$$Y = \{q, \ r\}$$

The Cartesian product of these two sets is the set of all ordered pairs that can be systematically constructed from their elements:

$$X \times Y = \{(x,y): x \in X \text{ and } y \in Y\}$$
$$= \{(a,q), \ (a,r), \ (b,q), \ (b,r), \ (c,q), \ (c,r)\}$$
$$Y \times X = \{(y,x): y \in Y \text{ and } x \in X\}$$
$$= \{(q,a), \ (q,b), \ (q,c), \ (r,a), \ (r,b), \ (r,c)\}.$$

Recall that $x \in X$ reads x is an element of X, and that $X \times Y$ consists of all elements denoted (x,y) where x is an element of X and y is an element of Y.[2]

Now, any subset of $X \times Y$ is a *binary relation*. Some possible binary relations defined on $X \times Y$ are:

$$\{(a,q), \ (c,q)\},$$
$$\{(a,q), \ (b,q), \ (c,q)\}, \text{ and}$$
$$\{(a,r), \ (b,r), \ (c,q), \ (c,r)\}.$$

(Z is a subset of T if every element of Z is an element of T.) Quite naturally, we can also define

$$X \times X = \{(x,y): x \in X \text{ and } y \in X\}$$

and speak of a binary relation on X (a subset of $X \times X$), such as the following:

$$\{(a,a), \ (b,b), \ (c,c)\},$$
$$\{(a,b), \ (b,c), \ (a,c)\}, \text{ and}$$
$$\{(c,a), \ (c,b), \ (c,c), \ (b,c), \ (a,c), \ (a,a), \ (b,b)\}.$$

Finally, a function from X into Y is a very special binary relation on $X \times Y$. In casual terms we think of $y = f(x)$ in which some $y \in Y$ is associated with each $x \in X$ using the rule $y = f(x)$. That is, to be a function there must be exactly one $y \in Y$ associated with any given

$x \in X$. This is a binary relation in which each $x \in X$ is in a single ordered pair from $X \times Y$.[3] The following binary relations are functions from X into Y:

$\{(a,q), (b,q), (c,q)\}$,
$\{(a,q), (b,q), (c,r)\}$,
$\{(a,q), (b,r), (c,q)\}$,
$\{(a,q), (b,r), (c,r)\}$,
$\{(a,r), (b,q), (c,q)\}$,
$\{(a,r), (b,q), (c,r)\}$,
$\{(a,r), (b,r), (c,q)\}$, and
$\{(a,r), (b,r), (c,r)\}$

while these are not:

$\{(a,q), (a,r), (b,q), (b,r)\}$,
$\{(b,q), (b,r)\}$, and
$\{(a,q), (b,r), (c,\pi)\}$.

Binary relations (on $X \times Y$) and functions (from X into Y), then, are subsets of $X \times Y$. Let **R** be a particular binary relation on $X \times Y$ and f a particular function from X into Y. Using the notation $(x,y) \in$ **R** or $(x,y) \in f$ is as cumbersome as it is technically correct, so we shorten the first to x**R**y and the second to $y = f(x)$. Another common notation for the function is $f: X \to Y$, read "f is a function from X into Y."

Armed with this terminology,[4] we now begin our study of information analysis.

FOOTNOTES

1. A more general view would interpret the signal as being transmitted to a set of decision makers. Explicit structural recognition of this class of problems is, however, beyond the scope of this book.
2. In turn (x,y) is an ordered pair in the causal sense that the specified order of the objects is important. We then have $(x,y) = (\bar{x},\bar{y})$ only when $x = \bar{x}$ and $y = \bar{y}$.
3. In more precise terms, let f be a subset of $X \times Y$. (We typically denote this by $f \subset X \times Y$.) f is a function from X to Y if there exists exactly one $(x,y) \in f$ for each $x \in X$.
4. Numerous references are available, such as Fishburn (1972) and Suppes (1972). A personal favorite is Earl (1963).

Chapter Two

EXPECTED UTILITY
REPRESENTATION

The purpose of this chapter is to study the assumptions that underlie our analysis of information. The key idea here is that our evaluator selects from among alternatives *as though* maximizing expected utility. Our basic goal in this chapter is to offer a precise statement of what this means as well as a set of assumptions that support such behavior.

A legitimate question at the outset is, "Why bother?" Several answers come to mind. It is, I think, important to reflect on the assumptions behind *any* analysis; the results of the analysis (if correctly obtained) are logical deductions of the assumptions. Moreover, these assumptions are likely to be somewhat unfamiliar. Most economic analysis assumes certainty, but to study the economic aspects of information, we must have uncertainty in our model. Hence, the economic analysis of uncertainty is the central idea. Maximizing expected utility is a cornerstone idea in the economic analysis of uncertainty. Finally, in a technical sense we measure preferences in a way that is useful in the study of information. Many study accounting systems as measures per se.[1] Here we alter this tack in a subtle way by measuring preferences over accounting measures. This allows us to ask what types of accounting measures are valuable, how they are used, and why they are valuable.

We begin with a motivating example. This is followed by a brief look at the technical meaning of measurement. We then apply this to measurement of preferences in two stages. First, we look at the case where no probabilities are present. Second, we introduce probabilities and thereby obtain the desired result of an individual behaving as though maximizing expected utility.

EXAMPLE

Suppose that a decision maker has decided to formally analyze the quality control aspects of a particular product. If the product meets specified quality standards, the decision maker would like to accept it; conversely, if it does not, the decision maker would like to reject it. The difficulty arises, of course, from not presently knowing whether the product meets the quality standards, and the decision maker must decide whether to accept or reject the product before such knowledge becomes available.

Example 9

Four different outcomes are possible. If the decision maker decides to accept the product, its quality could be (1) sufficient, or (2) inadequate. Similarly, if the decision is made to reject the product, its quality could also be (1) sufficient, or (2) inadequate. Let us assume that the decision maker is able to preferentially rank these four possible outcomes and express this ranking in an appropriate numerical fashion. We call the resulting numerical encoding of preferences a *utility function*. Exhibit 2.1 shows the specific utility measures for each conditional outcome for this example. Note that the two decision alternatives are labelled ACCEPT and REJECT and the two quality conditions CONFORM and NONCONFORM.

The decision maker would obviously prefer the ACCEPT, CONFORM outcome with a utility measure of 2 units, but does not have enough control to select this outcome. The decision maker can decide whether to accept or reject the product, but cannot control the quality. Put another way, the decision maker can select which gamble is preferable (ACCEPT or REJECT), but cannot select the outcome associated with either gamble. The ultimate outcome depends both on the choice and on which quality condition is actually present.

Uncontrollable determinants of outcome (in this case the level of quality) are generally called *states*. Many conceivable differentiations of states could be introduced, but it is economical to admit only those differentiations that are necessary for purposes of outcome differentiation. For example, quality in this case might refer to some physical dimension and the product might vary both with respect to this dimension and with respect to color. All conceivable alternatives of color and dimension could be introduced, but such a finely specified distinction is irrelevant. All the combinations of dimension and color for which the dimension satisfies the quality standard will result in identical utility measures for each act (because the decision maker is indifferent among them). Similarly, all the combinations of dimension and

Exhibit 2.1 Utility of conditional outcomes for example

| | | *Alternative states* | |
		CONFORM	NONCONFORM
Act choice by	ACCEPT	2	−4.0
decision maker	REJECT	0.1	1.0

color for which the dimension does *not* satisfy the quality standard will result in identical utility measures for each act.

The decision maker, then, does not know which state will occur, nor control the occurrence of a given state, but the decision maker does know which state *might* occur. Such knowledge could range from the nebulous to the very precise. Let us assume that this knowledge is expressed in terms of a probability function defined over the possible states; that is, the judgment of the decision maker is encoded in a probability function. In the present example, we assume a probability of 0.90 that CONFORM will occur and 0.10 that NONCONFORM will occur.

This completes the necessary specification. The decision maker has specified a list of alternative acts. Exactly one must be selected. Similarly, a list of uncontrollable determinants of outcomes or states has been specified. One and only one such state will occur. The decision maker's assessments of the respective possibilities of occurrence are expressed in an appropriate probability function. Finally, each conceivable relevant outcome, each possible combination of act and state, is described with an appropriate utility measurement. The only remaining task is one of computation.

Recall, now, that the expected value of the utility of a given act is defined to be the sum, over all possible states, of the utility of the conditional outcome (conditioned by a specific state and a specific act) multiplied by the probability of the specific state. Hence the expected value of utility of the ACCEPT alternative is

$$E(\text{ACCEPT}) = 2(0.90) - 4(0.10) = 1.40 \text{ units} \qquad (2.1)$$

and the expected value of utility of the REJECT alternative is

$$E(\text{REJECT}) = 0.1(0.90) + 1.0(0.10) = 0.19 \text{ units.} \qquad (2.2)$$

Clearly, then, the best alternative from an expected utility point of view is to ACCEPT, given the decision alternatives, states, probabilities, and utility of conditional outcomes specified.

Observe that the essential (and familiar) nature of the analysis in this example consists of (1) specifying the alternative acts, states, probabilities of states, and utility of conditional outcomes, and (2) selecting the act that will give the maximum expected utility. This decomposition of an uncertain choice situation into a preference encoding (the utility specification) and a likelihood encoding (the state probability specification) such that the decision maker's most preferred choice can be located by selecting the *maximum expected utility alternative* is the main contribution of decision theory. Our task here is to set forth the assumptions that lead to this result.

A BRIEF LOOK AT MEASURE THEORY

These assumptions are rooted in the notion of measuring the individual's preferences in a particular way. To fully appreciate this, we begin with a somewhat abstract look at the idea of measurement, or representation.

Measurement is, of course, a familiar idea. We use social security numbers to distinguish pension claimants, income to distinguish economic performance, current ratios to distinguish short run economic health, blood pressure to distinguish short run physical health, and so on. In each case we use numbers to tell us something about the objects of interest. In casual usage the numbers tell us what we seek to distinguish. But in theory we reverse this, pretend we have the objects distinguished, and seek a set of numerical assignments that will faithfully preserve or represent the distinguished objects! If it is indeed possible to construct such a set of numerical assignments, we then address the practical question of actually assigning the numbers to the objects.

This may strike you as perverse (at best). But it is important to understand that our casual use of measures belies the fact that logical existence of measures is not easy to come by. To illustrate, suppose I want to distinguish the beauty of three national parks, denoted *a*, *b*, and *c*. *a* is strictly more beautiful than *b*, *b* is strictly more beautiful than *c*, and *c* is strictly more beautiful than *a*. No set of beauty measures can be conjured up that will distinguish the parks in this manner. (Why?) Put differently, there does not exist a measure of beauty in this case.

The formal idea of measurement begins, then, with a set of objects, say A, that are distinguished in some manner. We catalogue, so to speak, the manner in which the objects are distinguished with a binary relation, say **R**, that is defined on A. (Remember that **R** is a subset of $A \times A$.) This set and associated relation is termed an *empirical relational system* (ERS), and is usually summarized with the imposing notation $\langle A, \mathbf{R} \rangle$. The empirical descriptor connotes the idea that in one way or another we have empirical (as opposed to conceptual) access to the elements in A and their relationship as captured by

R. For example, we have our three national parks, $A = \{a, b, c\}$ and a relation distinguishing their beauty, $\mathbf{R} = \{(a,b),(b,c), (c,a)\}$. ($a\mathbf{R}b$ denotes a is strictly more beautiful than b.)

Now envision a second relational system consisting of the set of real numbers, usually denoted $\mathbb{R}$, and a binary relation such as $>$, $=$, or $\geq$ thereon. We will focus on the ordering relation $\geq$. The resulting system $\langle \mathbb{R}, \geq \rangle$ is termed a *numerical relational system* (NRS).

Finally, consider a function that assigns a number to each element of A. Remember that the function assigns one and only one number to each element in A. Denote this function by $f(a) = r$ or f: $A \rightarrow \mathbb{R}$. We then say that the ERS is measured by the function f in the NRS if

for any $x,y \in A$ we have $x\mathbf{R}y$ if and only if we have $f(x) \geq f(y)$.

This is quite formal, but it has its purpose. The idea is to represent the relationship imbedded in **R** by assigning numbers to the objects so that the assigned numbers mirror that relationship. Return to our beautiful national parks. Some beauty index f, some function, must satisfy the following inequalities in this case:

NRS	ERS
$f(a) > f(b)$	$a\mathbf{R}b$ but not $b\mathbf{R}a$
$f(b) > f(c)$	$b\mathbf{R}c$ but not $c\mathbf{R}b$
$f(c) > f(a)$	$c\mathbf{R}a$ but not $a\mathbf{R}c$

Notice that this requires $f(a) > f(a)$, which is impossible; and this is why it was asserted that no measure of beauty exists in this case. Measurement is logically impossible.

On the other hand, if the beauty relation were such that a is strictly more beautiful than c we would have

NRS	ERS
$f(a) > f(b)$	$a\mathbf{R}b$ but not $b\mathbf{R}a$
$f(b) > f(c)$	$b\mathbf{R}c$ but not $c\mathbf{R}b$
$f(a) > f(c)$	$a\mathbf{R}c$ but not $c\mathbf{R}a$

and a measure of beauty would be readily available. Indeed, quite a few such measures would be available. See Exhibit 2.2.

Two important questions emerge. When does a measure *exist?* Granting existence, what can be said about the *uniqueness* of the mea-

Exhibit 2.2 Possible beauty measures

Park	f_1	f_2	f_3	f_4	f_5
a	3	8,000,000	0	8,169	.01
b	2	.1	− 5	8,168.2	.001
c	1	0	− 20	− 15,169	.0001

sure? The answers are to be found in the nature of the ERS. Suppose A is finite, meaning we can denote it by $\{a_1, a_2, \ldots, a_m\}$ for some particular integer m. We already have examples where with finite A measures do or do not exist, depending on the nature of the relation **R**.

This drives us to distinguish properties of the relation **R**. One important property is completeness. We say **R** is *complete* if any pair of elements in A can always be "compared" in the sense of **R**. More precisely, we say **R** is complete if for *any $a,b \in A$* we have a**R**b, b**R**a, or both. We also say **R** is *transitive* if for *any $a,b,c \in A$* a**R**b and b**R**c implies a**R**c; that is, **R** is transitive if whenever we have a**R**b and b**R**c we also have a**R**c.

These two properties of the empirical relation answer the existence question for finite A.

Theorem 1:[2] Let the ERS $\langle A,\mathbf{R} \rangle$ have finite A. Then there exists a measure of the ERS in $\langle \mathbb{R}, \geq \rangle$ if and only if **R** is complete and transitive.

Theorems of this type have a long history and wide application, being found in physics, psychology, economics, engineering, sociology, and even accounting. It should also be apparent that the Theorem is about the most elementary version we could offer, but it is sufficient for our purpose. It answers the question posed by our beautiful national parks example; A is finite, **R** is complete, but in the first case **R** is not transitive.

Finally, notice the nature of the logical conclusion offered. We begin with an ERS. If this ERS satisfies a list of properties, a measure exists. (Indeed, with A finite, existence of the measure is equivalent to **R** being complete and transitive; the literal meaning of "if and only if" is one of equivalence.) With these properties we are able to *represent* the relationship among elements of A depicted in **R** by the function f and the $\geq$ relation. That is, x**R**y in the ERS is equivalent to $f(x) \geq f(y)$ in the NRS.

Suppose we have eighty students rank ordered by size; Theorem 1 tells us it is possible to measure their size. Suppose we have the eighty students rank ordered by academic performance; Theorem 1 tells us it is possible to measure their performance. Suppose we have them rank ordered by age. Theorem 1 tells us it is possible to measure their age. Any ranking or complete and transitive enumeration of a finite set can be measured.

The other question of uniqueness also comes up here. Basically, Theorem 1 gives us ordinal measurement in that the function whose existence is guaranteed is unique up to strictly increasing transformation.[3] Our concern, however, is with the existence of a preference measure, so we will not discuss uniqueness in any detail.[4]

PREFERENCE MEASUREMENT WITHOUT PROBABILITIES

With this background, the notion of preference measurement should be easy to assimilate. We begin with the case in which no probabilities are involved in the measurement and merely apply Theorem 1.

Suppose a decision maker must select some act from the set $A = \{a_1, a_2, a_3, a_4\}$. We also assume our decision maker has a complete and transitive ranking of the alternatives. For illustrative purposes, assume the preferences are: a_4 strictly preferred to a_3, a_3 strictly preferred to a_2, and a_2 indifferent to a_1.

This ranking is readily expressed with the binary relation $\gtrsim$ in Exhibit 2.3. We interpret $a_4 \gtrsim a_3$ as meaning a_4 is at least as good as or ranked at least as high as a_3. You should check to be sure that $\gtrsim$ is complete and transitive.

Exhibit 2.3   Preference ranking on $\{a_1, a_2, a_3, a_4\}$

Pair of acts	Ranking
a_1 and a_1	$a_1 \gtrsim a_1$
a_1 and a_2	$a_1 \gtrsim a_2$ and $a_2 \gtrsim a_1$
a_1 and a_3	$a_3 \gtrsim a_1$
a_1 and a_4	$a_4 \gtrsim a_1$
a_2 and a_2	$a_2 \gtrsim a_2$
a_2 and a_3	$a_3 \gtrsim a_2$
a_2 and a_4	$a_4 \gtrsim a_2$
a_3 and a_3	$a_3 \gtrsim a_3$
a_3 and a_4	$a_4 \gtrsim a_3$
a_4 and a_4	$a_4 \gtrsim a_4$

Notice that $a_4 \gtrsim a_3$ but *not* $a_3 \gtrsim a_4$ connotes strict preference (which we denote by $a_4 > a_3$) while $a_1 \gtrsim a_2$ and $a_2 \gtrsim a_1$ connote indifference (which we denote by $a_1 \sim a_2$) in this scheme.

Now apply Theorem 1. A is finite. $\gtrsim$ is complete and transitive. Hence we know a measure exists. In fact, any numerical assignment satisfying the following inequalities does the trick:[5]

$$f(a_4) > f(a_3)$$
$$f(a_3) > f(a_2)$$
$$f(a_2) = f(a_1).$$

Examples are given in Exhibit 2.4.

We call such a function a *preference indicator*. When faced with choice of one $a \in A$ we know—given our knowledge of the decision maker's preferences—that a_4 will be selected in this case. And employing Theorem 1 we are able to say the decision maker behaves *as though* his or her preference indicator had been maximized.

How is this to be interpreted? The identified ERS of a set of choices and a complete and transitive preference ranking is sufficiently well structured to admit to measurement. Does the decision maker have such a measure? Surely the answer is yes. This is the importance of Theorem 1. Must the decision maker actually calculate the preference indicator? We don't know. All we know is that *if* those preferences are this well behaved, we can model the decision maker as having chosen $a \in A$ so as to maximize $f(a)$. If you have studied economics in any detail you will realize that being able to say little beyond the fact that an individual behaves as though having maximized $f(a)$ allows us to say a great deal about economic phenomena.

Further notice that we might reinterpret the setting in terms of the decision maker agreeing that invoking a complete and transitive ranking is a "desirable" way to proceed in life. Without completeness the concept of choice is ambiguous; we have noncomparable alternatives. Without transitivity, we would be admitting to a type of "money

Exhibit 2.4 Possible measures of $\langle \{a_1, a_2, a_3, a_4\}, \gtrsim \rangle$

element	f_1	f_2	f_3	f_4
a_1	1	5000	-8	10
a_2	1	5000	-8	10
a_3	2	5001	-7	13
a_4	3	18000	-6	15

pump." Our decision maker might, for example, prefer a_4 to a_3, a_3 to a_2, and a_2 to a_4 so much as to pay \$10 to switch from a_3 to a_4, another \$10 to switch from a_4 to a_2, and yet another \$10 to switch from a_2 to a_3—thereby winding up at the starting position less \$30! Most texts on decision theory take this view of offering systematic analysis, based on a preference indicator, as a "good" way to make choices. Inconsistencies are highlighted by such a procedure and the underlying assumptions are offered as a palatable foundation on which to proceed.[6] In a more conceptual sense, though, no claim of actual use is made. The measurement exists and is viewed as an equivalent model, as a representation, of the decision maker's choice behavior.

In any event, this is the meaning of the terminology "behaves as though his or her preference indicator had been maximized." This is not, however, a sufficiently rich description of choice behavior for our purpose of examining information. Our next step is to introduce and capitalize on the use of probabilities in the measurement. This will allow us to speak in terms of expected utility maximization.

PREFERENCE MEASUREMENT WITH PROBABILITIES

Any measure, in a technical sense, provides a representation of an ERS in a NRS. Use of probabilities in the measure must, therefore, have its roots in the ERS. So we must add more structure to our ERS if we are to produce a preference measure that uses probabilities.

The easiest way to proceed is to view the choice problem as we did in the motivating example in Exhibit 2.1, but with slightly more elaboration. In the original preference measurement example of Exhibit 2.4 with $A = \{a_1, a_2, a_3, a_4\}$, then, we now interpret each act as ultimately providing a cash flow. The eventual cash flow will depend on which act the decision maker selects as well as which uncontrollable event or state or act of Nature obtains. This state variable should be interpreted as a complete description of all determinants of the eventual cash flow outcome other than those controlled by the decision maker. (And in this sense the state should be viewed in a somewhat tautological fashion.)

Continuing the example, suppose two states are possible and denote them by s_1 and s_2. The actual cash flows are assumed to be those displayed in Exhibit 2.5.

Exhibit 2.5 Cash flow outcomes

		States	
		s_1	s_2
	a_1	$ 64	$144
Acts	a_2	$100	$100
	a_3	$324	$ 64
	a_4	$144	$324

If the decision maker selects a_3 and if state s_1 obtains, a cash flow of $324 will be realized. Also notice that the cash outcome is to be sharply distinguished from its utility. The latter is the measure we seek.

To produce this measure we will assume the state probability function exists and proceed in a somewhat roundabout fashion by focusing on a very rich set of gambles. This will provide the desired utility measure.

In particular, notice in the example in Exhibit 2.5 that the possible cash outcomes comprise the set $X = \{\$64, \$100, \$144, \$324\}$. In general the set of outcomes will be finite, and denoted $X = \{x_1, x_2, \ldots, x_n\}$. A very rich set of conceivable alternatives is now introduced. In particular, we consider the set of *all* gambles or lotteries over this specified set of outcomes, X. Denote this set of gambles by G. Typical elements in G are displayed in Exhibit 2.6.

Exhibit 2.6 Typical gambles on $\{\$64, \$100, \$144, \$324\}$

		Outcome Probabilities			
		$64	$100	$144	$324
	g_1	.25	.25	.25	.25
	g_2	.8	.1	0	.1
	g_3	0	0	1	0
Gambles	g_4	1	0	0	0
	g_5	.7	.1	.1	.1
	g_6	.3	.3	.2	.2

To fully appreciate the presumed richness of G, let us denote any particular element with the cumbersome notation $a = (a^1, a^2, \ldots, a^n)$. a^1 is the probability of receiving outcome x_1, a^2 is the probability of receiving outcome x^2, and so on. Quite clearly, the axioms of probability require that each $a^i \geq 0$ and that

$$\sum_{i=1}^{n} a^i = 1.$$

Hence G is the set of *all a* such that

$$\sum_{i=1}^{n} a^i = 1 \text{ and } a^i \geq \cdot 0 \text{ for } i = 1, \ldots, n.$$

G is, literally, the set of all conceivable gambles on the outcomes in X.

Now presuming a preference ranking on this very rich set of conceivable gambles provides the structure we seek. That is, we now use an ERS of $\langle G, \geq \rangle$. G is the set of all possible gambles over a given (finite) set of possible outcomes. $\geq$ is a preference ranking or binary relation on this set of gambles. We seek a measurement that exploits this probabilistic structure. Four axioms are used for this purpose.

1. Quite naturally we assume that the given preference ranking of gambles is complete and transitive. This means that our decision maker is able to compare all conceivable gambles over X and to do so in a transitive manner. Moreover, so-called degenerate gambles with $a^i = 1$ for some i are contained in G; so we are able to speak of comparing outcomes by comparing their respective degenerate gambles. Denote the degenerate gamble with guaranteed outcome x_i by $\bar{x}_i$. For convenience, we index the outcomes so that $\bar{x}_1 \geq \bar{x}_2 \geq \ldots \geq \bar{x}_n$.

Of course, nothing new is introduced here, relative to our initial preference measurement setting. In the abstract, we have a set of alternatives and a complete and transitive ranking thereof. (But Theorem 1 does not apply because G is not finite.) It is the remaining axioms that provide the expected utility measurement we seek.

2. Consider two gambles that involve only the best and worst outcomes, x_1 and x_n. In comparing these gambles the decision maker is assumed to prefer the gamble with the higher probability of producing x_1. For example, with possible cash outcomes of $X = \{\$400, \$100, \$1\}$ and more cash preferred to less, our decision maker is assumed to prefer $a = (.8, 0, .2)$ to $a' = (.7, 0, .3)$.

3. Suppose that we face a hybrid gamble in which one of the possible outcomes is a second gamble. We then assume that, through appropriate use of probability theory, we can redefine the first into the more basic uncertain outcomes of the second. For example, with $X = \{\$400, \$100, \$1\}$ we might envision a gamble based on the flip of a fair coin. If heads comes up, we play $a = (.8,0,.2)$ and if tails comes up we play $a' = (.7,0,.3)$. We assume such a gamble is completely equivalent to $a'' = (.75,0,.25)$—where the probability of obtaining $\$400$ is $.5(.8) + .5(.7) = .75$. Howard (1968) aptly refers to this as the "no-fun-in-gambling" axiom.

4. Consider any outcome $x_i \in X$. We assume there exists a probability such that the decision maker is indifferent between receiving x_i for certain (the degenerate gamble) or taking the gamble that produces the best outcome with probability $\hat{\phi}_i$ and the worst outcome with probability $1 - \hat{\phi}_i$—$(\hat{\phi}_i,0, \ldots 0,1 - \hat{\phi}_i)$. Quite naturally we call $\bar{x}_i$ the certain equivalent of $a = (\hat{\phi}_i, \ldots,1 - \hat{\phi}_i)$ and assume that $(\hat{\phi}_i,0, \ldots,0,1 - \hat{\phi}_i)$ and its certain equivalent can be substituted for one another in any gamble.

We formally state these four axioms in Exhibit 2.7. Their importance is summarized in the following result:[7]

Exhibit 2.7   Axioms for $\langle G, \gtrsim \rangle$ with $X = \{x_1, x_2, \ldots, x_n\}$

Definition: $G = \{(a^1, a^2, \ldots, a^n): \sum\limits_{i=1}^{n} a^i = 1,$ all $a^i \geq 0\}$

Convention: $\bar{x}_1 \gtrsim \bar{x}_2 \gtrsim \ldots \gtrsim \bar{x}_i$; where $\bar{x}_i \in G$ is the degenerate gamble at x_i.

Axiom 1: $\gtrsim$ is complete and transitive.

Axiom 2:   Consider $a,\bar{a} \in G$ with $a = (\phi,0, \ldots, 0,1 - \phi)$ and $\bar{a} = (\bar{\phi},0, \ldots, 0,1 - \bar{\phi})$. $a \gtrsim \bar{a}$ if and only if $\phi \geq \bar{\phi}$.

Axiom 3:   Let $\hat{a}$ consist of a "compound" gamble: a with probability ϕ and $\bar{a}$ with probability $1 - \phi$. $\hat{a} \sim (\phi a^1 + (1 - \phi)\bar{a}^1, \ldots, \phi a^n + (1 - \phi)\bar{a}^n)$

Axiom 4:   For each $i = 2, \ldots, n - 1$ there exists a probability $\hat{\phi}_i$ such that $\bar{x}_i \sim (\hat{\phi}_i,0, \ldots, 0,1 - \hat{\phi}_i)$; and the one is substitutable for the other in any gamble.

Theorem 2:   Suppose the ERS $\langle G, \geq \rangle$, based on a finite set of outcomes X, satisfies the preceding axioms 1 through 4. Then there exists a measure of the ERS in $\langle \mathbb{R}, \geq \rangle$. Moreover, this measure is the expected value of a function $U: X \rightarrow \mathbb{R}$.

Note carefully what we have here. As before, we measure $\langle G, \geq \rangle$ in $\langle \mathbb{R}, \geq \rangle$ via some function $f: G \rightarrow \mathbb{R}$. That is, $a \geq a'$ is equivalent to saying $f(a) \geq f(a')$. But $f(a)$ now has a quite special structure:

$$f(a) = \sum_{i=1}^{n} U(x_i)a^i$$

where $U(x)$ is to be interpreted as a utility function defined on (cash) outcomes.

Thus we have provided a system of choice under conditions of uncertain outcome in which the decision maker's preferred act can be located by selecting the act with the maximum expected value of utility. This utility function is merely an encoding of the decision maker's preferences; put another way, preference precedes utility. Moreover, the utility function is unique only up to a positive linear transformation. For any real numbers $\alpha > 0$ and β, $\beta U(x) + \alpha$ works just as well.[8] Thus, the utility measure can be used to establish preference rankings, but not to make interpersonal comparisons.

To illustrate this extended development, return to our example in Exhibit 2.5. Suppose Theorem 2 applies with $U(x) = \sqrt{x}$ and also assume the two states are equally likely. (Clearly $\{a_1, a_2, a_3, a_4\} \subset G$.) We therefore have

$$f(a_1) = \tfrac{1}{2}(\sqrt{64}) + \tfrac{1}{2}(\sqrt{144}) = 10$$
$$f(a_2) = \tfrac{1}{2}(\sqrt{100}) + \tfrac{1}{2}(\sqrt{100}) = 10$$
$$f(a_3) = \tfrac{1}{2}(\sqrt{324}) + \tfrac{1}{2}(\sqrt{64}) = 13$$
$$f(a_4) = \tfrac{1}{2}(\sqrt{144}) + \tfrac{1}{2}(\sqrt{324}) = 15$$

which should be compared with Exhibit 2.4.

This theorem, providing for the existence of an expected utility measure, is due to von Neumann and Morgenstern (1947). We interpret it in terms of the decision maker assessing probabilities and then exploiting these assessed probabilities in developing the desired expected utility measure. As you might suspect, a deeper treatment would entail measurement of these probabilities as well. But this is a deep, complicated subject; and the von Neumann-Morgenstern axiomatization is sufficient for our purposes.[9]

SUMMARY

Measurement is casually thought of in terms of numerically distinguishing objects. In formal terms it is a representation of an ERS in a NRS. Preference measurement, in turn, is associated with an ERS consisting of a set of choices and some preference ranking.

To describe a person's choice behavior in terms of maximizing expected utility, then, is to assert or assume that a particular measurement is possible. The identified choice behavior is logically equivalent to the (expected utility maximizing) model of that choice behavior. All this provides, as we shall see in the next chapter, a setting that has enough richness to examine information questions.

FOOTNOTES

1. Examples are Chambers (1965), Sterling (1970), Ijiri (1976), Mock (1976), and Abdel-Magid (1979). Beaver and Demski (1979) discuss the two approaches in a financial reporting context.
2. This Theorem dates back to the work of Cantor in the late nineteenth century and actually rests on a weaker assumption of countable A. To sketch the idea of the proof, first notice that existence of the measure directly implies $\mathbf{R}$ is complete and transitive because $\geq$ is a complete and transitive relation on the real numbers. Showing that $\mathbf{R}$ is complete and transitive implies existence is done by ranking the elements and assigning them their numerical rank (making sure to assign all ties the same value). That is, we number the elements so that $a_m \mathbf{R}\, a_{m-1} \mathbf{R} a_{m-2} \cdots \mathbf{R} a_1$. If all the elements are distinct in the sense we never have $a_{j-1}\, \mathbf{R} a_j$, merely assigning $f(a_j) = j$ provides the desired measure. If some elements are not distinct we assign them the same number, say the lowest index in the nondistinct group.
3. Strictly increasing means that $>$ is preserved. More formally, let g: $T \rightarrow \mathbb{R}$ where $T \subset \mathbb{R}$. Then g is strictly increasing if for any $x, y \in T$ with $x > y$ we have $g(x) > g(y)$.
4. Krantz et al. (1971) provide an extensive study of measure theory. An excellent introduction is offered by Coombs et al. (1970).
5. $a_4 \geq a_3$ requires $f(a_4) \geq f(a_3)$. But $\geq$ excludes $a_3 \geq a_4$ so the numerical assignments also exclude $f(a_3) \geq f(a_4)$. Hence $f(a_4) > f(a_3)$.

6. See Schlaifer (1969) or Holloway (1979).
7. The structure of the proof is easily seen by focusing on the special case of $X = \{x_1, x_2, x_3\}$. Axiom 1 allows us to adopt the ordering convention of $\bar{x}_1 \gtrsim \bar{x}_2 \gtrsim \bar{x}_3$. Axiom 4 allows us to set up the certain equivalent $\bar{x}_2 \sim (\hat{\phi}, 0, 1 - \hat{\phi})$ for some probability $\hat{\phi}$. Now consider any gamble $a = (a^1, a^2, a^3)$. We construct an equivalent compound gamble by substituting $(\hat{\phi}, 0, 1 - \hat{\phi})$ for the x_2 outcome. Then using Axiom 3 we readily have

$$a = (a^1, a^2, a^3) \sim (a^1 + a^2 \hat{\phi}, 0, a^3 + a^2 (1 - \hat{\phi})).$$

Do the same for

$$\bar{a} = (\bar{a}^1, \bar{a}^2, \bar{a}^3) \sim (\bar{a}^1 + \bar{a}^2 \hat{\phi}, 0, \bar{a}^3 + \bar{a}^2 (1 - \hat{\phi})).$$

Note that Axiom 2 ensures $a \gtrsim \bar{a}$ if and only if

$$a^1 + a^2 \hat{\phi} \geq \bar{a}^1 + \bar{a}^2 \hat{\phi}.$$

The trick is to capture this inequality with a utility measure. And using the probability of Axiom 4 does precisely this. We merely define $U(x)$ by:

$$U(x_1) = 1$$
$$U(x_2) = \hat{\phi}$$
$$U(x_3) = 0.$$

The resulting expected value is

$$f(a) = a^1 U(x_1) + a^2 U(x_2) + a^3 U(x_3)$$
$$= a^1 + a^2 \hat{\phi}$$

and we therefore have $a \gtrsim \bar{a}$ if and only if

$$f(a) = a^1 + a^2 \hat{\phi} \geq f(\bar{a}) = \bar{a}^1 + \bar{a}^2 \hat{\phi}.$$

8. We generally refer to this as a positive linear transformation. But in precise terms the transformation is affine.
9. This is, in fact, a summarization of the von Neumann-Morgenstern development. The interested reader should explore Kassouf (1970), Luce and Raiffa (1957), Anscombe and Aumann (1963), Savage (1954), Krantz et al. (1971), Fishburn (1970), Kreps and Porteus (1979), and Kreps (1979).

Chapter Three

ANALYSIS OF INFORMATION SYSTEMS

The purpose of this chapter is to explore the use and acquisition of information by a decision maker whose choice behavior can be described in terms of expected utility maximization. A subsequent chapter will extend the analysis to a setting in which the information evaluator and the decision maker are distinct individuals.

We begin with a statement of the decision maker's choice problem. Information is then introduced, and its use via consistent probability revision is examined. Finally, the decision maker's problem of selecting from among alternative information systems is discussed.

THE BASIC PROBLEM

We begin by formally stating the essential components of the decision maker's choice problem. Given that (1) the axiomatic structure reviewed in Chapter 2 is subscribed to, (2) the choice situation is recognized, and (3) formal analysis is decided to be worthwhile, the decision maker uses an existing level of experience to specify the following four facets of the problem.

1. The set of alternative resource commitments, decisions or *acts*. Let A denote this set and $a \in A$ one such specific act. One and only one $a \in A$ is to be selected.

2. The relevant set of *states*. Let S denote this set and $s \in S$ one such specific state. One and only one $s \in S$ will occur and S will always be regarded as a finite set. Moreover, the outcome or consequence of selecting a given $a \in A$ will likely depend on which $s \in S$ actually does occur. (Indeed, this property is the basis for deciding how to define the components of s and S.)[1]

3. A *probability* function that consistently describes the possibilities of the various states occurring. Denote this function $\phi(s)$ for $s \in S$.[2]

4. A set of *utility* assessments that preferentially describe the various possible outcomes in the choice situation. One can describe an outcome by specifying a unique combination of act and state. Hence to save notation the utility function previously described as being defined over the set of alternative outcomes is now viewed as being defined over the cartesian product of the sets S and A. That is, the utility of a given outcome is denoted $U(s,a)$, for all $s \in S$ and $a \in A$.

It remains quite essential that an outcome be distinguished from its utility. To force this distinction as well as to provide some convenience in addressing the meaning of the phrase "cost and value" of information, we will generally regard the outcome as a cash flow. $U(s,a)$, then, should be interpreted as the utility assessment of the cash flow that will result if act $a \in A$ is chosen and state $s \in S$ obtains.[3]

We can now locate the decision maker's most preferred decision or act by selecting the $a \in A$ with the largest expected value of utility. The expected utility from selecting act $a \in A$, which we denote $E(U|a)$, is given by

$$E(U|a) = \sum_{s \in S} U(s,a)\phi(s) \tag{3.1}$$

and the preferred or optimal act is the $a^* \in A$ that produces the maximum expected value.[4]

$$E(U|a^*) = \max_{a \in A} E(U|a) \tag{3.2}$$

Thus the decision maker's choice problem can be described by specifying the act set A, state set S, probability function ϕ, and utility function U. And, recalling that the decision maker specifies these facets on the basis of an existing level of experience, which we denote ξ, we shall call the set $\{A,S,\phi,U| \xi\}$ a *decision model*. For notational convenience, we shall often omit the conditioning ξ in our discussions, but its role remains paramount. For example, A does not contain all acts that the decision maker could take. Rather, it is restricted to those predicted to be possibly desirable, given the decision maker's experience. In the quality control example of Exhibit 2.1, for instance, it is conceivable that the decision maker could individually test each item before deciding whether to accept. But experience has led the decision maker to predict that such an alternative is not, without further analysis, desirable. Similarly, S does not contain an enumeration of all uncontrollable phenomena that could occur. Rather it is limited to a specification that is precise enough to effect the outcome differentiations that the experienced decision maker predicts will be desirable. To return to the quality control example, the decision maker differentiates all situations in which the physical dimension is sufficiently accurate from those in which it is not. Other differentiations are not made because, given current experience, the decision maker predicts that such differentiations would not be relevant for outcome specification.

If all four facets of the decision maker's model, $\{A, S, \phi, U| \xi\}$, are correctly specified, we call the model *complete*. "Correctly specified" here refers to the delineation the decision maker would make if specification and analysis were a free good. All conceivable alternatives would be included, and all conceivable necessary but uncertain outcome differentiations would be manifested in the state specification. Nothing of conceivable merit would be excluded from the model specification.

The notion of completeness does not, however, preclude error. Significant elements may be excluded simply because the decision maker is not aware of them. Product color in the quality control example of Exhibit 2.1 may ultimately turn out to be very important; and, if so, its suppression in the model constitutes an error. But we call the model correct because it contains all specifications perceived by the decision maker at the time of specification. Completeness, then, is an *ex ante* concept, dependent on the decision maker's level of experience, ξ. If ξ changes, the specification may change.

The completeness assumption is, of course, an unrealistic one, but it does give us a starting point for introducing the information considerations that we shall explore in this book. Specifically, if all facets of the model are correctly specified, the decision maker's outcome uncertainty is confined to state occurrence. That is, if the model is completely specified, the *ex ante* impact of information is limited to one of probability revision.

INFORMATION PROCESSING AND CHOICE
WITH A COMPLETE MODEL

Let us focus, then, on a specific decision maker employing a complete decision model. At this point, an optimizing act could be selected—the problem formulated in Eq. (3.2)—but we are specifically interested in analyzing the situation in which information is received after formulating the model, but before making a choice.[5] As mentioned, the completeness assumption is sufficient to guarantee that any information effects are strictly limited to probability revision.

Perfect information

To begin this exploration, suppose that a benevolent clairvoyant offers to reveal (at no cost whatever) the state that will ultimately occur. The clairvoyant will not err in this prediction (hence the term *perfect information*), and the prediction will be received before our decision maker must act. What will be done with such a revelation? Quite clearly, the decision maker will select the act that, in conjunction with the revealed state, produces the most desirable outcome—or largest $U(s,a)$.

Consider the example with states, acts, and $U(s,a)$ data presented in Exhibit 3.1. Three states are distinguished, with probabilities of $\phi(s_1) = .5$, $\phi(s_2) = .1$, and $\phi(s_3) = .4$.

Exhibit 3.1 State-act-utility data

		States		
		s_1	s_2	s_3
	a_1	100	20	120
Acts				
	a_2	110	90	90

If forced to chose without additional information, our decision maker will be indifferent between selecting a_1 or a_2:

$$E(U|a_1) = .5(100) + .1(20) + .4(120) = 100$$
$$E(U|a_2) = .5(110) + .1(90) + .4(90) = 100. \quad (3.3)$$

But with the clairvoyant's help, the decision maker will surely behave in the following manner:

Revealed state	Optimal act
s_1	a_2
s_2	a_2
s_3	a_1

which has an expected utility of

$$E(U|\text{perfect information}) = .5(110) + .1(90) + .4(120) = 112. \quad (3.4)$$

Observe the manner in which the decision maker processes the perfect state revelation from the clairvoyant. One of three messages will be received and, for each message, the decision maker may select a_1 or a_2. In effect, there are now eight alternative strategies for using the revelation: select a_1 no matter what, select a_2 no matter what, select a_1 if s_1 is revealed and a_2 otherwise, and so on. The implied choice structure is displayed in Exhibit 3.2.

Exhibit 3.2   Strategies with perfect information

Strategy	Act choice under			$U(s,a)$ under states			
	s_1	s_2	s_3	s_1	s_2	s_3	Expected utility
α_1	a_1	a_1	a_1	100	20	120	100
α_2	a_1	a_1	a_2	100	20	90	88
α_3	a_1	a_2	a_1	100	90	120	107
α_4	a_1	a_2	a_2	100	90	90	95
α_5	a_2	a_1	a_1	110	20	120	105
α_6	a_2	a_1	a_2	110	20	90	93
α_7	a_2	a_2	a_1	110	90	120	112
α_8	a_2	a_2	a_2	110	90	90	100

The optimal behavior is to select a_2 unless s_3 is revealed (strategy α_7). The point is that access to the clairvoyant's prediction allows the decision maker to vary choices as a function of that prediction. The choice problem thus becomes one of selecting among all functions that relate available acts to possible messages. (No randomization across the possible functions is entertained here; and a little thought should convince you that no such randomization would be useful.)

An equivalent, and more familiar, view of this is in terms of probability revision. If s_1 is revealed we surely have a revised probability of $\phi(s_1|\text{revelation of } s_1) = 1$. The clairvoyant's revelation, in other words, literally reduces the problem to one of choice under known outcome conditions. To fully appreciate this, let $\alpha(s)$ be any rule that assigns one and only one act $a \in A$ to each state $s \in S$. All such rules are available here because choice is postponed until the revelation is received. The decision maker will surely select the one that maximizes the expected utility:

$$E(U|\text{perfect information}) = \max_{\alpha(s)} \sum_{s \in S} U(s, \alpha(s))\phi(s)$$

$$= \sum_{s \in S} \phi(s) \{ \max_{a \in A} U(s,a)\}. \tag{3.5}$$

That is, the decision maker behaves as though (1) the revelation provides $\phi(s|\text{revelation}) = 1$ for the revealed state, and (2) then selects the act that maximizes $U(s,a)$ for that particular revealed state.

The quantity $E(U|\text{perfect information}) - E(U|a^*)$ is often termed the *expected value of perfect information*. It cannot be negative because the revelation is costless and (as should be clear from Exhibit 3.2) the decision maker can always choose to ignore it. This quantity is also often interpreted as an upper bound to the decision maker's gains to acquiring information. No such information could be better than perfect information and cost less than free information (assuming the decision maker is not paid to acquire the information). This is a subtle topic; and more will be said about it later.

Imperfect information

The case in which the decision maker receives some information, but such information does not perfectly reveal the state, is of course more common. Here we think in terms of movement from the prior probability $\phi(s)$ to the posterior or conditional probability, given the specific signal from the specific information system employed, $\phi(s|y,\eta)$.

But how does our decision maker move from $\phi(s)$ to $\phi(s|y,\eta)$? How is this information "processed"? Simply stated, this processing must be consistent with probability theory and, in particular, Bayes' rule.

Specific details will depend on the way the information system is modeled. For expositional reasons we adopt the convention associated with perfect information and assume the information system is such that one and only one signal is associated with each state. For our basic example in Exhibit 3.1 with three states, this allows for five conceivably different information systems. Let the possible signals be $Y = \{y_1, y_2, y_3\}$. Exhibit 3.3 displays the various possibilities.

Notice that η_1 is *null;* it tells the decision maker nothing. No matter what the state is, precisely the same message is obtained. Simi-

Exhibit 3.3 Possible information systems for $S = \{s_1, s_2, s_3\}$

	State		
	s_1	s_2	s_3
η_1	y_1	y_1	y_1
η_2	y_1	y_2	y_2
η_3	y_1	y_2	y_1
η_4	y_1	y_1	y_3
η_5	y_1	y_2	y_3

larly, η_5 is perfect. Also notice that other alternatives, other functions from S to Y, could be generated here by listing all possible rules that associate one and only one $y \in Y$ with each $s \in S$. But the five rules displayed in Exhibit 3.3 are all that matter. Any other rule is informationally equivalent to one of these. The essence of η_2 is that it distinguishes s_1 from s_2 *or* s_3. The essence of η_1 is it distinguishes nothing. The labels are irrelevant. In other words, reporting y_2 under s_1 and y_1 otherwise is informationally equivalent to η_2. Reporting y_3 no matter what is informationally equivalent to η_1; and so on.

With this descriptive convention, then, each information system is noiseless in the sense that one and only one signal or message is associated with each state. It is therefore possible to speak of the information system as a function: $y = \eta(s)$. The irrelevance of labeling is perhaps best noted by the fact that, in a technical sense, the information *partitions* or classifies the states in S.[6] If η_2 reports y_1 we know s_1 will obtain. If it reports y_2 we know s_2 or s_3 but not s_1 will obtain. Thus an equivalent view of the various information systems in Exhibit 3.3 associates the signals directly with the distinguished states. See Exhibit 3.4.

Further observe that this partitioning convention is perfectly general. Any "noise" associated with an information system is merely modeled by appropriate definition of the state variable.[7] While sometimes cumbersome in practice, this convention allows us to streamline our discussion of the conceptual nature of information.

Now let us examine our choice problem in Exhibit 3.1 when the decision maker costlessly receives the signal from η_2 in Exhibit 3.4. With two possible signals and two possible acts, there are now four possible strategies: select a_1 regardless of the signal, select a_2 regardless of the signal, select a_1 only if $\{s_1\}$ is observed, and select a_2 only if $\{s_1\}$ is observed. These possible uses of the information are summarized in Exhibit 3.5.

Exhibit 3.4   Possible partitions of $S = \{s_1, s_2, s_3\}$

Information system	Partition
η_1	$\{S\}$
η_2	$\{\{s_1\}, \{s_2, s_3\}\}$
η_3	$\{\{s_2\}, \{s_1, s_3\}\}$
η_4	$\{\{s_3\}, \{s_1, s_2\}\}$
η_5	$\{\{s_1\}, \{s_2\}, \{s_3\}\}$

Exhibit 3.5   Strategies with $\eta_2 = \{\{s_1\}, \{s_2, s_3\}\}$

Strategy	Act choice under		$U(s,a)$ under states			
	$y_1 = \{s_1\}$	$y_2 = \{s_2, s_3\}$	s_1	s_2	s_3	Expected utility
α_1	a_1	a_1	100	20	120	100
α_4	a_1	a_2	100	90	90	95
α_5	a_2	a_1	110	20	120	105
α_8	a_2	a_2	110	90	90	100

We see that the decision maker will select a_2 if $y_1 = \{s_1\}$ is received and a_1 otherwise. This has an expected utility of:

$$E(U|\eta_2) = .5(110) + .1(20) + .4(120) = 105. \tag{3.6}$$

Observe that the basic difference between perfect and imperfect information is the richness of the allowed behavior. With perfect information (Exhibit 3.2) our decision maker has available all rules that associate states with acts, but with imperfect information the decision maker is constrained to those rules that are consistent with the state partition at hand. Here, for example, the rule must be the same under s_2 and s_3 because η_2 does not allow these two states to be distinguished.

The jump from here to Bayesian probability revision is straightforward. Our decision maker wants to pick the best possible *available* strategy. Let $\alpha(y)$ be any strategy that is available here in the sense of the four distinguished strategies in Exhibit 3.5. We then have

$$E(U|\eta_2) = \max_{\alpha(y)} \{U(s_1,\alpha(y_1))\ \phi(s_1) + U(s_2,\alpha((y_2))\ \phi(s_2) +$$

$$U(s_3,\alpha(y_2))\ \phi(s_3)\}$$

$$= \phi(s_1)\{\max_{a \in A} U(s_1,a)\} + (\phi(s_2) + \phi(s_3))\cdot \tag{3.7}$$

$$\max_{a \in A} \{U(s_2,a)\ \frac{\phi(s_2)}{\phi(s_2)+\phi(s_3)} + U(s_3,a)\ \frac{\phi(s_3)}{\phi(s_2)+\phi(s_3)}\ \}.$$

Observe that with say y_2 observed, the definition of conditional probability provides:

$$\phi(s_2|y_2,\eta_2) = \frac{\phi(s_2)}{\phi(s_2)+\phi(s_3)}.$$

Hence, our decision maker behaves here as though, for each possible signal, beliefs are revised in a consistent fashion and the act is selected that maximizes the conditional expected utility measure.[8]

Finally, to state this in more general terms, consider information system η. This system might be costly so we now think in terms of $U(s,a,\eta)$—the utility of the cash flow if system η is used, act a is eventually selected, and state s obtains. Also, with $y = \eta(s)$ we have

$$\phi(y|\eta) = \sum_{\substack{s \in S \\ \text{such that} \\ y = \eta(s)}} \phi(s).$$

Having received signal y, the conditional probability is

$$\phi(s|y,\eta) = \begin{cases} \dfrac{\phi(s)}{\phi(y|\eta)} & \text{if } y = \eta(s) \\ 0 & \text{otherwise} \end{cases}$$

and the conditional expected value of utility with act a is

$$E(U|a,y,\eta) = \sum_{s \in S} U(s,a,\eta) \, \phi(s|y,\eta). \tag{3.8}$$

The maximum thereof is

$$E(U|y,\eta) = \max_{a \in A} E(U|a,y,\eta). \tag{3.9}$$

The expected utility associated with system η therefore is

$$E(U|\eta) = \sum_{y \in Y} \phi(y|\eta) \, E(U|y,\eta). \tag{3.10}$$

And system η_1 is at least as good as system η_2 if and only if

$$E(U|\eta_1) \geq E(U|\eta_2). \tag{3.11}$$

Additional examples

Additional examples may be a welcome relief at this juncture. For reasons that will become clear later in the chapter, we continue with the same basic example of three states, two acts, and a costless information system (η_2) that distinguishes s_1 from s_2 or s_3. Recall that the state probabilities are $\phi(s_1) = .5$, $\phi(s_2) = .1$, and $\phi(s_3) = .4$. Only the $U(s,a)$ assessments differ.

First consider the utility assessments in Exhibit 3.6. The decision maker will, if forced to choose without additional information, select a_2:

$$\begin{aligned} E(U|a_1) &= .5(10.00) + .1(4.47) + .4(10.95) = 9.83 \\ E(U|a_2) &= .5(10.49) + .1(9.49) + .4(9.49) = 9.99 \end{aligned} \tag{3.12}$$

Exhibit 3.6 State-act-utility data

		States		
		s_1	s_2	s_3
Acts	a_1	10.00	4.47	10.95
	a_2	10.49	9.49	9.49

But if η_2 in Exhibit 3.4 is accessible, the decision maker has the four alternative strategies displayed in Exhibit 3.7, and we clearly have

$$E(U|\eta_2) = .5(10.49) + .1(4.47) + .4(10.95) = 10.07. \qquad (3.13)$$

Exhibit 3.7 Strategies with $\eta_2 = \{\{s_1\}, \{s_2, s_3\}\}$

Act choice under		U(s,a) under states			
$y_1 = \{s_1\}$	$y_2 = \{s_2, s_3\}$	s_1	s_2	s_3	Expected utility
a_1	a_1	10.00	4.47	10.95	9.83
a_1	a_2	10.00	9.49	9.49	9.75
a_2	a_1	10.49	4.47	10.95	10.07
a_2	a_2	10.49	9.49	9.49	9.99

Second, consider the utility assessments in Exhibit 3.8. You should verify that the preferred act without additional information is a_2 ($E(U|a_2^*) = 3.16$) and that the optimal use of η_2 is to always select a_2. In other words, η_2 is *useless* in this setting. Though the probabilities are revised, the act does not change. Hence, we have $E(U|\eta_2) = E(U|a_2^*)$. (Indeed, you should also verify that the identified strategy in each example maximizes $E(U|a,y,\eta_2)$ for each signal.)

Exhibit 3.8 State-act-utility data

		States		
		s_1	s_2	s_3
Acts	a_1	3.16	2.11	3.31
	a_2	3.24	3.08	3.08

COST AND VALUE OF INFORMATION

Our basic utility measure of an information system is given in Eq. (3.10). Nothing is said here in terms of cost or value, yet familiar terminology and more popular treatments of the subject use this language. Can we, then, re-express Eq. (3.10) in cost and value terms such that one system is better than another if the value less cost of the first exceeds the value less cost of the second?

As you might expect, the answer is at best a highly qualified yes. Recall that outcomes are, for convenience, being interpreted as cash flows. Further suppose for the moment that our decision maker maximizes expected cash flow (being risk neutral). Let $f(s,a)$ denote the cash flow if act a is selected and state s obtains. Also let $C(\eta)$ be the cost of acquiring and using system η. Quite clearly, then, $U(s,a,\eta) = f(s,a) - C(\eta)$. Moreover,

$$E(U|y,\eta) = \max_{a \in A} \sum_{s \in S} [f(s,a) - C(\eta)] \, \phi(s|y,\eta)$$

$$= \max_{a \in A} \sum_{s \in S} f(s,a) \, \phi(s|y,\eta) - C(\eta). \tag{3.14}$$

Hence

$$E(U|\eta) = \sum_{y \in Y} \phi(y|\eta) \{ \max_{a \in A} \sum_{s \in S} f(s,a) \, \phi(s|y,\eta) \} - C(\eta). \tag{3.15}$$

The first term could be thought of as a value measure and the second is surely a cost measure; so with risk neutrality or expected cash flow maximization our desired cost and value representation is readily available.

Unfortunately, this simple construction and interpretation depends on a linear utility function. Suppose the utility assessment for net cash flow is nonlinear, implying $U(s,a,\eta) = U(f(s,a) - C(\eta))$ with $U(\cdot)$ nonlinear. Then no such separability is evident and must be forced. In this case a so-called *buying price* is often focused on by locating the maximum fixed price k that the decision maker would pay for the information system:

$$E(U|a^*) = \sum_{y \in Y} \phi(y|\eta) \{ \max_{a \in A} \sum_{s \in S} U(f(s,a) - k) \, \phi(s|y,\eta) \}. \tag{3.16}$$

In turn, system η is not too expensive if its "value" k exceeds its cost, $C(\eta)$. This is all well and good *and* agrees with the value measure in Eq. (3.15) with a linear (or risk neutral) utility function. The difficulty is that $k_1 > k_2$ does not imply $E(U|\eta_1) > E(U|\eta_2)$, even with $C(\eta_1) = C(\eta_2)$. This unhappy state of affairs occurs because k measures the maximum amount our decision maker would pay for η relative to no information while the question being asked concerns comparison across various information systems.

An alternative is to focus on a so-called *selling price* (or certain equivalent), by locating the minimum fixed amount our poor decision maker would *sell* the choice problem (complete with η) for:

$$U(\hat{k}) = E(U|\eta). \tag{3.17}$$

And we always have $\hat{k}_1 > \hat{k}_2$ if and only if $E(U|\eta_1) > E(U|\eta_2)$. From here it is a short but obvious step to re-express $\hat{k}$ as a value less cost measure and we have the desired result. The only difficulty is its cumbersome nature. It is, in many respects, a re-expression of the $E(U|\eta)$ measure in Eq. (3.10). So I, personally, disfavor the cost-value terminology and relegate it to the realm of casual conversation.[9]

GENERAL RANKINGS

A remaining concern in our exploration of information systems is whether more general statements can be made. It is a bit unfortunate that all of this work has produced only the statement that η_1 is as good as η_2 when $E(U|\eta_1) \geq E(U|\eta_2)$. On the other hand, we are not generally accustomed to saying one computer system is better than another for all situations, one graduate school is better than another for all situations, or one bag of groceries is better than another for all families.

The difficulty, of course, is that individual circumstances and tastes are important determinants of desirability. The same holds for information systems. Information is, in a broad sense, a factor of production; it is used to improve the quality of decisions. And the alternatives, tastes, and beliefs at hand are important determinants of the desirability of one information system versus another.

Examine again the three examples in Exhibits 3.5, 3.6, and 3.8. Each deals with the same states, acts, and costless information structure. The first actually is a case in which $U(s,a) =$ cash flow, the second has $U(s,a) = (\text{cash flow})^{1/2}$, and the third has $U(s,a) = (\text{cash flow})^{1/4}$. Moreover, the optimal use of the information in the third case is to totally ignore it. No matter what the message, our decision maker will continue to select a_2 in this case. Just by varying the utility assessments, in other words, we are able to create situations in which the desirable becomes useless. (What actually happens here is the decision maker becomes sufficiently risk averse in the third case to avoid the a_1 gamble even when s_2 or s_3 will obtain.)[10] Indeed we could go further and show that the optimal use of information may vary with how much that information costs.[11]

All is not lost, however. Let us confine the discussion to costless information systems. Otherwise we could always reverse a ranking by increasing the cost of the higher ranked system by a sufficient amount. Turn back to Exhibits 3.2 and 3.5. These Exhibits list all alternatives available to our decision maker under each of two information systems. Notice that everything available in Exhibit 3.5 is also available in Exhibit 3.2. This is a key idea.

Suppose we fix S and consider *all* choice problems for which S is the set of states. All A, $U(s,a)$ and $\phi(s)$ are considered here. Now consider two costless information systems, η_1 and η_2; when will we have $E(U|\eta_1) \geq E(U|\eta_2)$ regardless of available acts, beliefs, and $U(s,a)$ assessments? If the options available under η_1 are always available under η_2, we will surely have $E(U|\eta_1) \geq E(U|\eta_2)$. It costs nothing (by assumption) to switch from η_2 to η_1. And everything you can do with η_2 you can also do with η_1 (and possibly more).

Moreover, this notion can be expressed as a property of the information systems themselves. We earlier made the observation that with our modeling convention each information system partitions S. One system, η_1, one partition of S, will provide all of the options that another, η_2, will if the first is a *subpartition* of the second. Intuitively, this means that η_1 either "passes on" the message from η_2 or "subdivides" it. Another way to state this is to say that the messages from η_2 can be expressed as a function of those from η_1. In yet more formal terms, η_1 subpartitions η_2 if each element in the η_1 classification scheme is a subset of one of those in the η_2 scheme. Consider Exhibit 3.4. η_5 subpartitions each of the other systems; and η_2, η_3, and η_4 each subpartition η_1. Also notice that η_2, η_3, and η_4 are not comparable in the subpartitioning sense. (η_2 does not subpartition η_3, η_3 does not subpartition η_2, and so on.)

Theorem 3:[12]   Fix the set of states S and consider two costless information systems thereon, η_1 and η_2. $E(U|\eta_1) \geq E(U|\eta_2)$ for all choice problems defined on S if and only if η_1 is a subpartition of η_2.

In other words, saying that costless η_1 ranks as good as costless η_2 in every decision makers' eyes (for some specified S) is equivalent to saying that η_1 subpartitions η_2. If η_1 does subpartition η_2, anything available under η_2 remains available under η_1. If η_1 does not subpartition η_2 and η_2 does not subpartition η_1, we can construct a choice problem on S for which $E(U|\eta_1) > E(U|\eta_2)$, and yet another one for which $E(U|\eta_2) > E(U|\eta_1)$.

This result implies that costless perfect information never "hurts": $E(U|\text{perfect information}) \geq E(U|a^*)$. Either you use it (a strict gain) or ignore it. Also notice that any attempt to study information by focusing on the properties of the information systems per se must be based on the subpartitioning relationship if it is to be consistent with the general notion of expected utility maximization. This applies to attempts to study accounting alternatives in terms of properties such as relevance and objectivity, or communication channels in terms of their entropy.[13] Perhaps more important is the narrowness of the Theorem. It says that more is better than less, at zero cost. Other than this, comparison of even costless information systems must reflect the choice problem at hand. General rankings remain in the realm of fiction.

SUMMARY

Analysis of information systems follows quite directly from the dual assumptions of a completely identified choice problem and choice behavior described by expected utility maximization. Processing of any message or signal is done in a consistent, Bayesian revision fashion. This, in turn, provides for a straightforward utility calculation for comparing alternative information systems.

Though this utility measure can be interpreted in cost and value of information terms, that interpretation is in general rather cumbersome. The utility measure is also quite essential to our continued study of information because even costless information systems can be compared without resort to the specifics of the choice problem at hand only in a narrow class of systems where the subpartitioning relation holds.

In turn, introduction of the cost of analysis generally results in a model that is less than complete. In this case, information may have an impact far beyond that of systematic probability revision. In the following chapter we explore this altered role of information in the context of an incomplete (or simplified) model.

FOOTNOTES

1. Specification of the appropriate partition over all future states depends on the outcome situation perceived by the decision maker. If it is perceived that future weather differences are important in differentiating among outcomes, then alternative weather states will be included in S; otherwise they will not. See Marschak (1963). Also, as in the act set, s may be interpreted as a vector.

2. Let E denote any subset of S. We term E an *event*. A function ϕ, defined over all events, is a probability measure if it satisfies the following three properties:

   Axiom 1: $0 \le \phi(E)$ for any event E.

   Axiom 2: $\phi(S) = 1$.

   Axiom 3: $\phi(E_1 \cup E_2) = \phi(E_1) + \phi(E_2)$ if E_1 and E_2 are mutually exclusive events.

   Elaboration is available in Parzen (1960) and Fishburn (1970).

3. With this cash flow orientation we are also able to say something about the decision maker's attitude toward risk. Let x denote the cash flow outcome.

   Suppose the decision maker's utility is a (positive) linear function of x. Recalling the uniqueness of this utility measure we can just as well use $U(x) = x$. The decision maker behaves as though maximizing expected cash flow. Moreover, the decision maker is indifferent between participating in a 50-50 gamble over winning $1000 or nothing and receiving $500 for certain:

   $$500 = \tfrac{1}{2}(1000) + \tfrac{1}{2}(0).$$

   Contrast this with the case where $U(x)$ is strictly concave or displays decreasing marginal utility. A ready example is $U(x) = \sqrt{x}$. For the same gamble as above we have

   $$\sqrt{500} = 22.36 > \tfrac{1}{2}\sqrt{1000} + \tfrac{1}{2}\sqrt{0} = 15.81.$$

   Indeed, we would have to pay this decision maker $125 to engage in such a gamble:

   $$\sqrt{500} = 22.36 = \tfrac{1}{2}\sqrt{1125} + \tfrac{1}{2}\sqrt{125}.$$

   The first decision maker is said to be *risk neutral* while the second is *risk averse*. See Pratt (1964) for an extensive discussion.

4. We naturally assume that such a maximum exists; this assumption is maintained throughout the book.

5. An alternative view of our discussion at this point is that the complete model has been formulated without any information alternatives and we are now introducing them.

6. Let $G = \{g_1, g_2, \ldots, g_m\}$ be a set of subsets of S. We say G partitions S if the elements of G (1) cover S ($g_1 \cup g_2 \cup \ldots \cup g_m = S$), and (2) are pairwise disjoint ($g_i \cap g_j = \Phi$ for all $i \neq j$).

7. Suppose we have two states, s_1 and s_2, and three signals, y_1, y_2, and y_3, with the following "noisy" structure:

Focus on the obvious Cartesian product: $S \times Y = \{(s_1,y_1), (s_1,y_2), (s_1,y_3), (s_2,y_1), (s_2,y_2), (s_2,y_3)\}$. Letting this set be the choice problem's basic set of states allows us to view the information system as partitioning the set of states, via $\{\{(s_1,y_1)\}, \{(s_2,y_2)\}, \{(s_1,y_3), (s_2,y_3)\}\}$—where we have dropped the two obviously impossible events of $\{(s_1,y_2)\}$ and $\{(s_2,y_1)\}$.

8. In more precise language, let y (from η) be any subset of S with

$$\phi(y|\eta) = \sum_{s \in y} \phi(s) > 0.$$

Then the conditional probability of s given y (from η) is defined to be

$$\phi(s|y,\eta) = \begin{cases} \dfrac{\phi(s)}{\phi(y|\eta)} & \text{for all } s \in y \\ \\ 0 & \text{otherwise.} \end{cases}$$

Alternatively, let B and C be subsets of S, both of which have nonzero probability. By definition, we have

$$\phi(B|C) = \frac{\phi(B \text{ and } C)}{\phi(C)}$$

and

$$\phi(C|B) = \frac{\phi(B \text{ and } C)}{\phi(B)}.$$

Hence

$$\phi(B|C) = \frac{\phi(C|B)\phi(B)}{\phi(C)}$$

which is Bayes' rule.

We therefore describe the individual's information processing behavior in term of consistent, Bayesian probability revision:

$$\phi(s|y,\eta) = \frac{\phi(y|s,\eta)\phi(s)}{\sum\limits_{s\in S} \phi(y|s,\eta)\phi(s)} = \begin{cases} \dfrac{\phi(s)}{\phi(y|\eta)} & \text{for } y = \eta(s) \\[2ex] 0 & \text{otherwise} \end{cases}$$

for $\phi(y|\eta) > 0$ (and $\phi(y|s,\eta)$ is clearly 0 unless $y = \eta(s)$).

9. The following example, due to Marschak and Radner (1972) is illustrative. Four equally likely states and five acts are present along with the following cash flows:

	s_1	s_2	s_3	s_4
a_1	1	0	-100	-100
a_2	-100	-100	1	0
a_3	.4	-100	.4	-100
a_4	-100	.4	-100	.4
a_5	0	0	0	0

The decision maker's utility for cash flow x is given by

$$U(x) = \begin{cases} x & \text{for } x \le \tfrac{1}{2} \\[1ex] .2x + .4 & \text{for } x \ge \tfrac{1}{2} \end{cases}$$

And two costless information systems are present:

$\eta_1 = \{\{s_1,s_2\}, \{s_3,s_4\}\}$ and $\eta_2 = \{\{s_1,s_3\}, \{s_2,s_4\}\}$.

We readily determine $E(U|a_5^*) = 0$, $E(U|\eta_1) = .3$, and $E(U|\eta_2) = .4$. Moreover, selling prices are $\hat{k}_1 = .3$ and $\hat{k}_2 = .4$ while buying prices are $k_1 = .5$ and $k_2 = .4$!

Also notice that buying and selling prices agree with one another under linear $(U(x) = x)$ or negative exponential $(U(x) = -e^{-x/C}$ where $C > 0)$ utility functions. This has a natural interpretation in terms of constant risk aversion. See La Valle (1968) for an extensive discussion, including attention to regularity issues that we have not addressed here.

10. Gould (1974) and Laffont (1976) explore the relationship between "value" of information and risk aversion. Also see LaValle (1968), Kihlstrom (1974, 1974a), Ohlson (1975), Ponssard (1975), Wilson (1975), Grossman et al. (1977), Itami (1977), Merkhofer (1977), and Hilton (1979, 1979a).

11. To see this, rework the $U(s,a) = $ (cash flow)$^{\frac{1}{2}}$ case, assuming the cost of η_2 is $20.

12. This Theorem is an application of a compendium of results popularly re-
    ferred to as Blackwell's Theorem. The original impetus was the compari-
    son of statistical experiments. McGuire (1972) and Marschak and
    Miyasawa (1968) should be consulted for an extensive treatment of the
    subject. Marschak and Radner (1972) provide an intermediate treatment.
    Accounting applications are to be found in Feltham (1972, 1977),
    Marshall (1972), Demski (1973a), Warren (1974), Demski and Feltham
    (1976), and Patell (1979).

    The structure of the proof should be clear from the text. First, suppose η_1
    subpartitions η_2 and denote the respective signals by y_1 and y_2. This pro-
    vides:

    $$E(U|\eta_2) = \sum_{y_2 \in Y} \phi(y_2|\eta_2) \, E(U|y_2,\eta_2)$$

    $$= \sum_{y_2 \in Y} \sum_{y_1 \subset y_2} \phi(y_1|\eta_1) \, E(U|y_2,\eta_2)$$

    $$\leq \sum_{y_2 \in Y} \sum_{y_1 \subset y_2} \phi(y_1|\eta_1) \, E(U|y_1,\eta_1)$$

    $$= E(U|\eta_1).$$

    Second, suppose $E(U|\eta_1) \geq E(U|\eta_2)$ for all choice problems, but η_1 does
    not subpartition η_2. A contradiction can be constructed along the follow-
    ing lines for the case of four states:

    | | Problem 1 | | | |
	s_1	s_2	s_3	s_4
a_1	1	1	0	0
a_2	0	0	1	1

    | | Problem 2 | | | |
	s_1	s_2	s_3	s_4
a_1	1	0	1	0
a_2	0	1	0	1

    Let the states be equally likely and consider $\eta_1 = \{\{s_1,s_2\}, \{s_3,s_4\}\}$ and
    $\eta_2 = \{\{s_1,s_3\}, \{s_2,s_4\}\}$. We clearly have $E(U|\eta_1) > E(U|\eta_2)$ in Problem 1
    but $E(U|\eta_2) > E(U|\eta_1)$ in Problem 2.

13. We can be more negative here. Focusing on costless information systems,
    preference of η_1 over η_2 for all problems (with S fixed) is equivalent to η_1
    subpartitioning η_2. Now apply Theorem 1. The subpartitioning relation is
    incomplete. Hence no measure of preference that is dependent on only
    the properties of the systems themselves can exist. Radner (1972),
    Marschak and Radner (1972), and McGuire (1972) discuss this. Its impor-
    tance in accounting is examined in Feltham (1972) and Demski (1973a,
    1976).

SIMPLIFIED DECISION ANALYSIS

The purpose of this chapter is to relax the completeness assumption so heavily relied on in the information analyses in Chapter 3. In the process we shall discuss the manner in which less-than-complete models are usually constructed, the resulting altered role of information in such a model, and the use of sensitivity analysis as a simplified or less-than-complete information analysis device.

SIMPLIFIED MODELS

The cost of decision analysis generally precludes use of a complete model by the decision maker; less-than-complete, or simplified, models are the rule.[1] Moreover, alternative simplifications, or alternative models, generally exist. For example, in an inventory model, the question of whether to express the cost of stockouts as a function of the number of stockouts, the length of time stockouts exist, or both is really a question of which model is more appropriate. Similarly, the question of whether to introduce learning effects in a production scheduling model is really a question of which model is more appropriate. In a broad sense, then, specification of the model is itself a decision.[2]

Choice of a simplified model

Because of the complexity of these issues, however, the process of specification of the model is usually approached in a heuristic manner. That is, the decision maker usually uses "rules of thumb" based on experience, as opposed to formal analyses, to determine the degree of complexity to include in (or exclude from) the model. Similarly, the decision maker usually uses rules of thumb based on experience to determine the amount of research to do in a given decision situation in order to determine some of the basic inclusion-exclusion alternatives.

Basically, this typical approach is an iterative process consisting of two major steps or phases of (re)specification and test. The decision maker begins by using current experience to construct an initial model of the real process. This model, of course, is an abstraction that reflects the decision maker's present knowledge, as well as numerous simplifying assumptions.[3] For example, in order to use a linear programming formulation, we often assume a linear technology relationship. This assumption is usually incorrect, but the real situation may be sufficiently close to linearity so that the assumption provides a useful basis for predicting the real system's dynamics.[4] Similarly, we often assume that a given cost or technology coefficient is known with certainty, when in fact few really are. Such assumptions simplify the model considerably; and, if actual variations from the predictions are relatively small, the predictions made possible by use of the model can be very useful.

In addition to simplifying relationships, the decision maker often achieves further abstraction by ignoring various relationships or phenomena altogether. For instance, in predicting the outcome associated with various decision alternatives, we often ignore future-period effects. Many production scheduling models ignore the future-period effects of present schedule alternatives. Similarly, hierarchical effects within an organization are also often ignored. Many production and marketing decisions, despite their obvious interdependencies, are made in a semiautonomous manner.

Exhibit 4.1 depicts the situation we have described. The vertical axis represents hierarchical effects and the horizontal axis represents future time period effects. If we included all relevant phenomena, we would have a model that covered all the white space in the large box. But the typical simplified model includes only a portion of these phenomena, as the shaded box indicates.

This is not to imply, however, that the typical model is not useful, or even that it is not as useful as it could be. Inclusion of more phenomena would add a nontrivial cost to the decision process. Furthermore, in constructing the model, the decision maker tries to balance the predicted "value" of improved decisions against the pre-

Exhibit 4.1 Complete versus simplified model

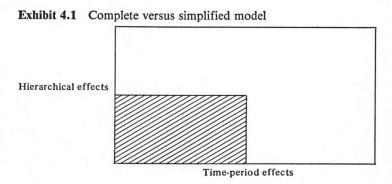

Hierarchical effects

Time-period effects

dicted "cost" of improved decision models. This leads us to the sec-ond·major step in the process of constructing a typical model.

Once a model has been proposed (step 1), it is subjected to test. Basically, the decision maker wants a model that will adequately rank the various acts. In the attempt to do this, the decision maker often uses various tests to determine whether the model adequately predicts the real system's perceived dynamics. For example, one test technique that is apparently very useful is sensitivity analysis. In this sort of analysis, the decision maker tries to determine the change in the model's act selection or expected utility that would result from a given change in one of the model's assumptions, or set of assumptions. If the change is small, the assumption is presumably relatively insignifi-cant. If, however, the change is considerable, the assumption is pre-sumably quite significant. We shall say more about this role of sensi-tivity analysis in a subsequent section.

Finally, on the basis of these tests, the decision maker decides whether to accept the model or refine it and subject it to additional testing. The entire process is depicted in Exhibit 4.2.

One might, at this juncture, question the wisdom of specifying, or constructing, the decision model in this heuristic fashion, without formal decision analysis of alternative models. That is, why do we generally proceed in the fashion described and not by formally consid-ering alternative models, states, and related outcomes? The answer is simple, if we are willing to go along with the rationale of extant modeling practices. This implies that the process of specifying the

Exhibit 4.2   Typical process of specifying and testing a model

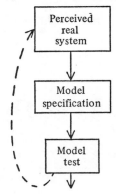

model is so complex (that is, costly) that mere heuristic search for a satisfactory model usually results in a better combination of model and analysis cost than would rigorous decision analysis of alternative models.

Thus the simplified decision model actually employed is likely to be the product of an evolutionary, heuristic process of model specification. Let us now formally characterize such a model.

The resulting simplified model

Successful simplification is a little-understood art.[5] The types of simplifications employed appear to be largely limited by the decision maker's imagination. Thus we shall not present an exhaustive discussion of the subject, but merely an interpretative framework, or model.

Simplification of act specification.   To begin, consider the decision maker's specification of perceived choices. Usually individual acts are not specified with anywhere near the detail presumed in the complete model. Some classes of acts are excluded altogether. Most control activities fall into this category. Similarly, short run output models assume fixed facilities; and capital-investment models typically assume given output decisions.

Other classes of acts are implicitly included in the simplified model. Individual machine schedules and supporting raw-material inventory schedules, for example, are implicitly included in the typical product-mix model. Once we determine an aggregate schedule, we can determine the appropriate machine and raw-material inventory schedules. We say that such classes of decisions are implicit in the simplified model because they are subsequently determined with reference to the schedule of the more aggregate model.[6]

Thus most models avoid a detailed representation of the complete act and rely on a less-detailed *decision variable representation*. We denote this variable d.

Simplification of state specification.   In a similar manner, most simplified models avoid the state differentiations reflected in the complete model. Consequences in a future period of decisions made in a current period are often imperfectly represented. For example, one often views advertising as having an effect that decreases with the passage of time (represented by its predicted effect on some mythical average consumer), without explicitly including its effects on individual customers. Similarly, choices as to the quality of a product are usually made without explicit reference to the effect which that quality will have on individual customers. Other possible aspects are ignored altogether. The typical inventory model does not take into account the possibility that a natural disaster might occur which would keep the supplier from meeting a delivery schedule. Similarly, output determination models usually fail to include either the reactions of competitors or breakdowns of individual machines.

We interpret this movement from a more-detailed to a less-detailed representation of a state as replacing the state $s \in S$ specification with a *parameter specification,* $\theta \in \Theta$. Machine failures, for example, are not given detailed representation but are introduced by way of an average-capacity parameter.

Simplification of the probability function. The less-detailed parameter specification $\theta \in \Theta$ may be derived from the state specification, $s \in S$. In this case, one could obtain the necessary $\phi(\theta)$ assessments by using $\phi(s)$ and the relationship between S and Θ. This is not, however, the likely case. Some components of θ may be regarded by the decision maker as certain and/or independent when, in fact, the contrary is perceived. Similarly, when recognizing uncertainty, the decision maker may assume that a standard distribution, such as the normal or beta distribution, characterizes likelihood judgments; and suppression of uncertainty, as well as most uses of standard distributions, requires inconsistent information processing.[7]

Simplification of the utility assessment. Recall that complete utility specification depends on the outcomes and that outcomes are, in turn, dependent on the choice of act as well as the occurrence of a given state. Hence simplification of acts and states may be viewed as a process of developing an approximate relationship among acts, states, and outcomes. Simplification does not, however, stop at this point. The utility measurement itself is often simplified. A risk neutral expected value of cash flow objective is often employed; and, literally interpreted, such a measurement of utility would mean that a person would display complete indifference between a certain outcome of $100,000 and a 50-50 chance of winning $200,000 or nothing. Similarly, when we introduce considerations of risk, approximate expressions are the rule. The mean-variance utility measure of risk analysis is a ready example.

We call the simplified measurement of utility an *objective function*. Recalling the specifications of the decision variable d and the parameter θ, we denote the objective function $R(\theta,d)$.[8]

Restrictions on decision variables. Finally, the set of admissible decision variables is often explicitly constrained. Such restrictions may be designed to rule out values of decision variables that are truly impractical (the use of balance equations is an example), or these restrictions may result from simplifications. The decision maker may elect to ignore those values of decision variables considered undesirable. Similarly, as part of the process of utility simplification, the decision maker may introduce constraints. For example, if utility is regarded as a linear function of the decision variables over a limited range, the decision maker would then establish constraints to ensure that they would be contained within the specified range. Alternatively, if uncertainty is recognized, the decision maker may regard utility as a linear function of the cash flow, so long as adequate liquidity (or other) levels are maintained.[9]

We summarize these constraints by requiring the decision variable to be a member of the set $D(\theta,\phi)$—a set of available alternatives that depends on the parameters and their predicted values.

Statement of the simplified model. The decision maker's simplified model is thus expressed in terms of decision variables, parameters, probabilities, constraints, and an objective function. It takes the following form, where $E(R|d^*)$ denotes the decision maker's maximum expected return:

$$E(R|d^*) = \max_{d} \sum_{\theta \in \Theta} R(\theta,d)\phi(\theta)$$

subject to $d \in D(\theta,\phi)$.   (4.1)

Thus the model the decision maker actually employs is likely to be a less-than-complete specification of the choice problem. The decision maker is likely to exclude some act components; of those included some are not likely to be entirely consistent with the individual's preferences and likelihood judgments. Two implications emerge. First, the optimal decision, d^*, cannot, strictly speaking, be regarded as the decision maker's preferred choice. Rather, it must be interpreted as information. Not completely having encoded his or her perceptions in the model, the decision maker cannot, strictly speaking, delegate choice selection to the model. Hence the optimal decision determined by means of the simplified model is one—but not necessarily the only—determinant of the decision maker's ultimate choice. Second, less-than-complete encoding in the simplified model ensures that the effects of some *ex ante* information may have an impact beyond the parameter probabilities and may, indeed, be "extra-model" in nature (that is, they may occur outside the domain of the simplified model). We shall discuss this altered role of information in the following section. We conclude the present section with an example.

Example

Consider a classic product mix problem with two possible products. The decision maker suppresses all choice possibilities (including expansion of facilities, individual machine scheduling, inventory considerations, maintenance schedules, and work force alterations) except the level of production for the two final products. We denote these d_1 and d_2. Two production departments with limited capacity are employed. The decision maker assumes a linear technology relationship in each and formulates the following simplified linear programming model:

$$E(R|d^*) = \max_{d_1, d_2 \geq 0} \theta_1 d_1 + \theta_2 d_2$$
$$\text{subject to } \theta_3 d_1 + \theta_4 d_2 \leq \theta_5$$
$$\theta_6 d_1 + \theta_7 d_2 \leq \theta_8. \tag{4.2}$$

We observe that, for modeling purposes, fractional outputs of either product have been regarded as feasible.

All uncontrollable phenomena are, of course, imbedded in the parameter specifications. The θ_5 and θ_8 capacity parameters, for example, reflect the machine time that is available, and thus abstract from or average over specific machine failure possibilities. Similarly, the technology coefficients (θ_3, θ_4, θ_6, and θ_7) reflect, among other things, some form of average time of processing. The decision maker regards $\theta_3, \ldots, \theta_8$ as certain, but explicitly recognizes contribution margin uncertainty for each product. The particular $\theta_3, \ldots, \theta_8$ specifications are displayed in Eq. (4.2a), and the contribution margin assessments are given in Exhibit 4.3. (Independence is assumed.)

Exhibit 4.3 Decision maker's contribution margin probability assessments
Contribution margin

	10	15	20
$\phi(\theta_1)$	½	¼	¼
$\phi(\theta_2)$	¼	½	¼

In spite of these formal probability assessments, however, the decision maker ignores risk considerations in the objective function and merely uses expected values for θ_1 and θ_2 in Eq. (4.2). Hence the choice model, with specific parameter values, is

$$E(R|d^*) = \max_{d_1, d_2 \geq 0} 13.75 \; d_1 + 15 \; d_2$$
$$\text{subject to } 1d_1 + 1d_2 \leq 400$$
$$1d_1 + 2d_2 \leq 500. \tag{4.2a}$$

The optimal solution is $d_1^* = 300$ and $d_2^* = 100$ with $E(R|d^*) = 5625$.

THE ALTERED ROLE OF INFORMATION

The decision maker consciously selects a simplified model and knowingly develops an approximate expression of the choice problem. Hence it is conceivable that the receipt of some signal y from some information system η might cause the decision maker to alter more than just the probability assessments. Such alterations could also occur with a complete model after the fact; but they are not conceivable before the fact because the complete model embraces all phenomena which the decision maker is able to perceive at the time of specification. Recognition of a simplified model, on the other hand, implies, by virtue of its simplification, that the decision maker has consciously suppressed various phenomena. Hence it is conceivable, before the fact, that information may have an impact beyond the probability assessments.

To better appreciate this, consider a situation in which the decision maker structures the planning horizon into a sequence of decision periods and employs a well-defined simplified decision model to determine the optimal values of the decision variables at the start of each

Exhibit 4.4   Complete versus simplified model act inclusions

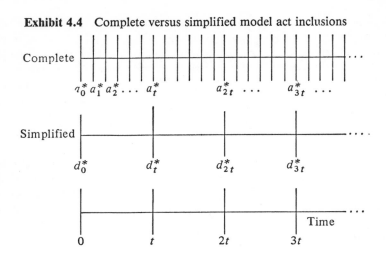

such decision period. Exhibit 4.4 shows this type of situation; the subscripts refer to time. With a complete model all possible acts would be analyzed in excruciating detail, and the act component chosen at any particular instant would reflect all available information up to that point as well as the prospect of receiving additional information in the future. (Remember, such analysis is a free good in a complete model.) With a simplified model (recognizing the cost of analysis) the story is quite different. Limited analysis will be engaged in, on a less frequent basis. The items of information will still be received and choices will still be made, but in a less formal manner.

For example, information might be received daily, and thus anyone wishing to perform complete analysis would have to carry out a formal analysis of daily acts. With a simplified model, however, the decision maker might do formal analyses weekly or monthly, and use less formal, *ad hoc,* extramodel analyses to process daily information and make necessary choices.[10]

Thus we see that, between two successive points at which formal analysis by means of a simplified model takes place, decision activity proceeds at two levels. First, information may indicate that action should be taken to alter the anticipated implementation of that portion of the original decision that has not yet been implemented. For example, suppose that d_0^* reflects a weekly production schedule. Information received at midweek might indicate that the schedule for the remainder of the week should be changed, that errors in implementation (i.e., errors in carrying out acts selected at the beginning of the week) should be rectified, or both. Second, information might also indicate that the simplified model or implementation subsystem should be changed.[11] For example, the information may indicate the desirability of a change in forecasting procedures or the methods used to motivate supervisors of the production department.

Exhibit 4.5 gives another view of this activity. At the beginning of some decision period, the decision maker makes a set of predictions based on experience, combines these with the ("best") decision model, and determines an optimal decision.[12] We call this process *planning*. After the initial implementation of these plans, the decision maker observes various events, and these observations provide a basis for *control* of the implemented decision. These post-decision observations go to make up what is called *feedback information*. This information supports extramodel or control decisions, such as deciding whether to intervene at some point, whether to alter the original schedule, whether to alter the simplified model, and so on.[13] Feedback information thus provides a basis for adapting or evolving the model,

Exhibit 4.5   Information-(simplified) decision model interactions

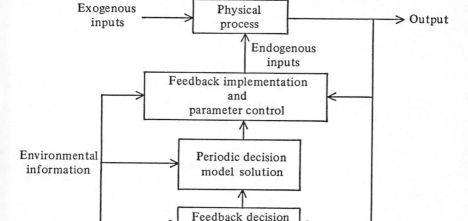

as well as altering the current decision. Indeed, it is easy to conceive of another level in this hierarchy, designed to control this control system, and so on. Thus, a simplified approach to the decision maker's problem provides a planning-control view of his choice behavior.

Planning centers around specifying all facets of the simplified model and required predictions in order to determine the optimal values of the decision variables for the next decision period. Control consists of the dual processes of implementation adaptation and model change as feedback information is received.

Such a description, in turn, allows us to say something about the role of information in a simplified decision analysis. First, notice that many (control) components of the choice problem are likely to be dealt with outside of whatever formal (planning) model is used. Hence focusing on the simplified model allows for but a partial view of how the decision maker might use the information.[14] Second, the information's impact on the formal model may be much more extensive than one of consistent parameter probability revision (in a Bayesian fashion). Due to their simplified nature, it is conceivable to the decision maker that receipt of some message might induce alteration of the parameter predictions (perhaps in a nonBayesian fashion), as well as the objective function or the constraint set.

To emphasize this altered role of information, suppose we ignore extramodel considerations and focus exclusively on the planning model. Recognizing the potentially broad impact of information, the expected return after receipt of signal y from system η would be

$$E(R|d^*,y,\eta) = \max_d \sum_{\theta \in \Theta} R(\theta,d,|y,\eta) \; \phi(\theta|y,\eta)$$

$$\text{subject to } d \in D(\theta,\phi|y,\eta). \tag{4.3}$$

With a complete model, the signal-impact is confined to movement from $\phi(s)$ to $\phi(s|y,\eta)$; and this movement is accomplished via Bayesian probability revision. Here, however, the movement may be much more extensive; and the manner in which it is accomplished is problematic to say the least. It might be highly formalized, as in the case of exponential smoothing or explicit Bayesian revision, or it might be entirely subjective.

We may, however, make additional formal explorations if we further limit the effect of additional information to the revision of probabilities. This is the topic of sensitivity analysis.

SIMPLIFIED INFORMATION ANALYSIS
USING SENSITIVITY ANALYSIS

Suppose, then, that we limit the effect of additional information to the revision of probabilities (or the prediction of parameters) in some particular simplified planning model. As a starting point in focusing on the question of information choice under these more limited conditions, we often find sensitivity analysis. Two basic forms are used.

The first poses the question of how the *optimal* value of the objective function varies as the parameter predictions are varied. The decision variables are optimally adjusted in this procedure and, for this reason, Howard (1971) refers to it as *closed-loop sensitivity analysis*. This type of sensitivity analysis is very common in linear programming applications. To illustrate its fundamental nature, suppose that we fix some component of θ, say θ_1 at the value of $\hat{\theta}_1$. Then the resulting maximum expected return, $E(R| \hat{\theta}_1, d(\hat{\theta}_1)^*)$, is determined by

$$E(R| \hat{\theta}_1, d(\hat{\theta}_1)^*) = \max_d \sum_{\theta \in \Theta} R(\theta, d)\phi(\theta| \hat{\theta}_1)$$

$$\text{subject to } d \in D(\theta, \phi| \hat{\theta}_1). \tag{4.4}$$

Subsequently ranging $E(R| \hat{\theta}_1, d(\hat{\theta}_1)^*)$ over some specific set of values, say $\hat{\theta}_1 \in \hat{\Theta}_1$, produces the desired result of indicating how the optimal value of the objective function varies as the parameter predictions are varied.

The second method poses the question of how the value of the objective function associated with a *fixed* decision varies as the parameter predictions are varied. If we focus on the original optimal decision in Eq. (4.1), d^*, but fix θ_1 at $\hat{\theta}_1$, the resulting expected return, $E(\hat{R}| \hat{\theta}_1, d^*)$, would be:

$$E(\hat{R}| \hat{\theta}_1, d^*) = \sum_{\theta \in \Theta} \hat{R}(\theta, d^*)\phi(\theta| \hat{\theta}_1), \tag{4.5}$$

where $\hat{R}(\theta, d^*)$ is a (possibly augmented) objective function capable of assessing the impact of an infeasible d^*. That is, d^* satisfies the constraints as originally formulated, but fixing θ_1 at $\hat{\theta}_1$ may alter the constraint set, and thus may render d^* infeasible. If this is the case, we must formally introduce the impact of such infeasibility into the analysis.[15] Howard (1971) refers to this as *open-loop sensitivity analysis* because the decision is not altered as the parameter information is introduced. And ranging $E(\hat{R}| \hat{\theta}_1, d^*)$ over $\hat{\theta}_1 \in \hat{\Theta}_1$ provides the desired analysis.

These two basic computations provide a basis for simplified information analysis by the decision maker. In particular, suppose it is revealed that $\hat{\theta}_1$ will obtain. Without such information, d^* will be chosen, while with such information $d(\hat{\theta}_1)^*$ will be chosen. The effect of such revelation, in units of expected return, is the difference between the closed- and open-loop calculations:[16] $E(R|\hat{\theta}_1, d(\hat{\theta}_1)^*) - E(\hat{R}|\hat{\theta}_1, d^*)$. In turn, taking expectations over Θ_1 provides an indication of the maximum amount, in units of return, the decision maker would pay for revelation of θ_1 before making a decision:

$$\sum_{\theta_1 \in \Theta_1} E(R|\theta_1, d(\theta_1)^*)\phi(\theta_1) - \sum_{\theta_1 \in \Theta_1} E(\hat{R}|\theta_1, d^*)\phi(\theta_1), \qquad (4.6)$$

where, of course, $\phi(\theta_1)$ denotes the probability of observing $\theta_1 \in \Theta_1$. This computation is a direct parallel to the expected value of perfect information developed in Chapter 3. Recognizing the simplifying assumptions, however, we interpret it only as an indication of the expected value of revelation.

Thus sensitivity analysis provides a basis for information choice by the decision maker under simplified-model conditions.[17] But since the analyses depend on a simplified model (indeed, *there is no reason for performing sensitivity analyses when a complete model has been specified*), they only provide indications of the desirability of various information proposals; and, as indicated, they are often conducted in a strict *ceteris paribus* fashion that abstracts from parameter interactions.[18]

Example 1

To illustrate some of these computations, return to the linear programming example in Eq. (4.2), and ask how much the decision maker would be willing to exchange for revelation of the first product's uncertain contribution margin, θ_1. Recall that in the absence of new information the decision maker will select $d_1^* = 300$ and $d_2^* = 100$. Subsequent revelation that θ_1 is either 10 or 15 will not alter this decision (assuming strict independence between θ_1 and θ_2). However, if the decision maker finds out that $\theta_1 = 20$, the decision will be altered to $d_1(20)^* = 400$ and $d_2(20)^* = 0$. At this point the value of the optimal expected objective function is $400(20) + 0(15) = 8000$, while the value associated with the original decision is

$$E(\hat{R}|20, d^*) = 300(20) + 100(15) = 7500.$$

Exhibit 4.6 shows the open- and closed-loop sensitivity results.

Exhibit 4.6   Example 1: Open- and closed-loop sensitivity analyses

Parameter value	Open-loop result $E(\hat{R}|\theta_1,d^*)$	Closed-loop result $E(R|\theta_1,d(\theta_1)^*)$
$\theta_1 = 10$	4500	4500
$\theta_1 = 15$	6000	6000
$\theta_1 = 20$	7500	8000

To complete the calculations implied in Eq. (4.6), we use the various conditional expected objective function values in Exhibit 4.6 and the original probability specifications in Exhibit 4.3. Thus

$$4500(\tfrac{1}{2}) + 6000(\tfrac{1}{4}) + 8000(\tfrac{1}{4})$$

$$- 4500(\tfrac{1}{2}) - 6000(\tfrac{1}{4}) - 7500(\tfrac{1}{4}) = 125,$$

which, as mentioned above, provides an indication of the maximum amount the decision maker would be willing to exchange for the information.

Example 2

To illustrate the infeasibility problem alluded to in the open-loop calculation, again consider the basic problem in Eq. (4.2) but now focus on the θ_5 capacity parameter. For purposes of discussion, we also assume $\theta_1 = 13.75$ and $\theta_2 = 15$, just as in Eq. (4.2a). Now suppose the θ_5 parameter will be 350, 400, or 450 with respective probabilities of $\tfrac{1}{3}$, $\tfrac{1}{3}$, and $\tfrac{1}{3}$. The sensitivity analyses are presented in Exhibit 4.7.

Consider the closed-loop results. If $\theta_5 = 350$, the optimal solution is $d_1(350)^* = 200$ and $d_2(350)^* = 150$. Similarly, for $\theta_5 = 450$, we have $d_1(450)^* = 400$ and $d_2(450)^* = 50$. And of course $d_1(400)^* = 300$ and $d_2(400)^* = 100$. Difficulty arises, however, with the open-loop

Exhibit 4.7   Example 2: Open- and closed-loop sensitivity analyses

Parameter value	Open-loop result $E(\hat{R}|\theta_5,d^*)$	Closed-loop result $E(R|\theta_5,d(\theta_5)^*)$
$\theta_5 = 350$	?	5000
$\theta_5 = 400$	5625	5625
$\theta_5 = 450$	5625	6250

computation. With $d_1^* = 300$ and $d_2^* = 100$, we have no difficulty when $\theta_5 = 400$ or when $\theta_5 = 450$, but $\theta_5 = 350$ is another story. Here the demanded capacity is $1(300) + 1(100) = 400 > \theta_5 = 350$. That is, with $\theta_5 = 350$ the $d_1^* = 300$ and $d_2^* = 100$ decision is infeasible. It is not allowed. The model cannot (*by construction*) evaluate or predict the consequences of such an occurrence.

To close the analysis we must, as implied in Eq. (4.5), change the model. Assume, then, that in such a case the firm will produce ($d_1^* = 300$ and $d_2^* = 100$) as planned and will purchase extra capacity in the local spot market at a price of $10 per unit. This implies

$$\hat{R}(\theta,d) = \begin{cases} 13.75\ d_1 + 15\ d_2 - 10(d_1 + d_2 - \theta_5) \\ \qquad \text{if } d_1 + d_2 \geq \theta_5 \\ \\ 13.75\ d_1 + 15\ d_2 \quad \text{otherwise} \end{cases}$$

Hence, with $\theta_5 = 350$ we have $E(\hat{R}|350,d^*) = 5625 - 10(50) = 5125$. And an indication of the maximum amount our decision maker would be willing to exchange for θ_5 revelation is thus provided by

$$\tfrac{1}{3}(5000) + \tfrac{1}{3}(5625) + \tfrac{1}{3}(6250)$$
$$- \tfrac{1}{3}(5125) - \tfrac{1}{3}(5625) - \tfrac{1}{3}(5625) = \tfrac{500}{3}.$$

Notice, as a final comment, that if outside purchase of θ_5 capacity is available here, the original formulation in Eq. (4.2) is questionable. Indeed it is possible for the information value datum to be negative because of the simplified exclusion of capacity expansion alternatives in the original model!

SUMMARY

Complete decision analysis is so complex that decision makers usually use less-than-complete models on which to base their analyses. This raises three points of interest in our study of information. First, alternative simplifications exist; and model specification itself is thus viewed as a decision. Second, the decision maker does not, strictly speaking, delegate selection of the act choice to the simplified model, although selection would be delegated to the complete model. Rather, the optimal decision determined by the simplified model is a form of information. When a model is simplified, it loses its conceptual clarity of a preference and likelihood encoding that leads to an arithmetization of the decision maker's choice problem. Third, in a simplified model, information issues may expand far beyond those of the revision of probabilities. In turn, confining the information issues to systematic parameter revision allows, using familiar sensitivity techniques, for calculation of a simplified information "value" measure.

FOOTNOTES

1. We take the existence of simplified models as a given in this chapter and interpret them as partial analyses that arise because of the cost of analysis. Schlaifer (1969), Simon (1972), Eilon (1974), Demski and Feltham (1976), and Holloway (1979) provide extensive discussion of this view. Coombs et al. (1970), Libby and Fishburn (1977), Keen and Scott-Morton (1978), and Mock and Vasarhelyi (1978) should be consulted for alternative views.

2. See Smallwood (1968) for a formal analysis of the choice of a model when completeness is desired but when the specific nature of the model is uncertain.

3. Howard (1968) describes this phenomenon in terms of a model "space" reflecting the basic dimensions of complexity.

4. See Ijiri (1965) and Baumol and Bushnell (1967) for a discussion of linear approximation. Also see Avriel and Williams (1970) and Huang et al. (1977) for an exploration of linear approximation in information value calculations.

5. See Ackoff (1962), Morris (1967), and U.S. General Accounting Office (1979) for further discussion.

6. See Holt et al. (1960), Chase and Aquilano (1977), and Buffa and Miller (1979) for extensive discussion of simplified approaches to analyzing the firm's production problems. Lee and Khumawala (1974) and Eilon (1975) address the question of selecting from among these alternative models. And to fully appreciate the simplifications present here, the scheduling work of Nelson et al. (1977) and Holloway et al. (1979) should be examined.

7. By "inconsistent information processing" I mean probability revision that does not follow Bayes' rule. Harrison (1977) discusses the problem of "calibration error" in assessing $\phi(\theta)$ and points out that with such error independence is highly unlikely. Each event potentially tells you something about the calibration error and hence about all other possible events.

8. See Hertz (1964). Further notice that numerous accounting issues arise here. So-called relevant costs, for example, are sufficient for analysis if $R(\cdot)$ is linear. Otherwise, outcome components that do not vary with d may be important in assessing the riskiness of the alternatives at hand. See Demski and Feltham (1976) and Dillon and Nash (1978). In a similar

vein, accounting measures are often relied upon in the specification of $R(\cdot)$—cost allocations provide numerous examples. Again, see Demski and Feltham (1976).

9. And if the decision maker did not perceive that explicitly introducing the effects of inadequate liquidity was worthwhile, a chance constraint would likely be used, a constraint whose probability of maintenance would have to equal or exceed some externally specified probability. In this liquidity illustration, the constraint would take the form of requiring the probability of maintenance of liquidity to equal or exceed some specified lower bound.

10. These extramodel analyses may be based on a formal control model with a very limited scope, but they are, in fact, removed from the decision maker's basic simplified model.

11. The word *implementation,* as used here, refers to all acts undertaken in order to effect the chosen alternative. It includes such mundane issues as the specification, scheduling, and coordination of minute activities, as well as instructing those who perform them. Thus, when we speak of altering an implementation subsystem, we mean altering the process by which choices are implemented. These issues do not attract specific attention in a complete model because they are formally included in the model, but in a simplified model they are items that are generally not taken into account.

12. Strictly speaking, d^* is determined by optimization of the model in Eq. (4.1); act components not explicitly considered in the model would be determined by some extramodel method.

13. That is, the function of feedback is not necessarily to ensure conformity to a static plan, or to an original decision. Feedback allows for revision of the original decision.

14. Of course we might also employ a formal control model. (See Kaplan's (1975) survey paper.) In turn we could consider further simplifications of this simplified control model, as in Magee (1976) and Dittman and Prakash (1979). Also notice that with simplified analysis and information processing it is conceivable that errors can be made. Ackoff's (1967) notion of management "misinformation" is an example.

15. Since constraint issues are subsumed in this $\hat{R}(\cdot)$ specification, the constraints are not included in Eq. (4.5). Further observe that θ_1 may not alter any of the constraints. An objective-function parameter in a linear program is one such example. Moreover, this issue of formally recognizing constraint violations is central to the two-stage optimization approach of linear programming under uncertainty. See Wagner (1975).

16. See Demski (1967) for an analysis of an accounting system that reports this measure—the difference between what the firm could have earned (with perfect information) and what it did earn, where calculations are based on a simplified planning model.

17. Precisely the same ideas are involved in formally analyzing whether to include a specific decision variable directly in the model. To illustrate, recall the vector nature of d, and consider the effect of deleting element d_1 from the model. Once deleted, d_1 would be set at either some constant

amount or some amount dependent on the optimal values of the other decision variables included in the model. We may functionally express either situation with the constraint $g(d) = 0$.

Thus

$$E(\mathrm{R}|d_1,d^{**}) = \max_{d} \sum_{\theta \in \Theta} R(\theta,d)\phi(\theta)$$
$$\text{subject to } d \in D(\theta,\phi)$$
$$g(d) = 0,$$

and $E(R|d^*) - E(R|d_1,d^{**})$ is an indication of the reduction in return resulting from the specified implicit determination of the d_1 element (where we assume d_1 to be feasible).

18. See Demski (1968) for further discussion of the limitations of sensitivity analysis.

Chapter Five

PRODUCER-USER SEPARATION

The purpose of this chapter is to examine the evaluator's particular decision, selection of an information system. Since this is a choice problem, the preceding discussion is applicable. The only additional complexity we shall introduce is to make a distinction between the person who selects the information system, the *information evaluator,* and the person who uses the output of that system, the *decision maker.*

Distinguishing between the information evaluator and the decision maker is, of course, important when they are separate individuals, which is common in most large organizations. The controller, for example, often selects accounting systems whose data are transmitted to separate decision makers. Similarly, in a firm with a number of divisions, transfer pricing mechanisms are usually established at the central level but employed by decision makers at the divisional level. Distinction between the information evaluator and the decision maker is also useful when the two roles are performed by the same person, but with simplified models. In such a case, cost-effective simplifications vary with the decision problem; and structural distinction between choice of an information system and subsequent use of information (in other decisions) once again becomes desirable.

We begin with a simple motivating illustration and then proceed to a formal statement of the evaluator's choice problem. We then present an additional illustration, and conclude with a discussion of information and simplification as they relate to the task of the information evaluator.

EXAMPLE

Consider the example given in Chapter 2 (page 9) in which a decision maker tries to determine whether to accept or reject a given product. The utility evaluation of the conditional outcomes is repeated in Exhibit 5.1.

Exhibit 5.1 Conditional outcome evaluations

| | | Alternative states | |
		CONFORM	NONCONFORM
Act	ACCEPT	2	−4.0
alternatives	REJECT	0.1	1.0

Example   65

Recalling his probabilities of 0.90 for the CONFORM and 0.10 for the NONCONFORM state, the decision maker will select the ACCEPT alternative because its expected utility exceeds that of the REJECT alternative. That is

$$E(U|\text{ACCEPT}) = .9(2) + .1(-4) = 1.40 > E(U|\text{REJECT}) =$$
$$.9(0.1) + .1(1) = 0.19. \tag{5.1}$$

Moreover, access to costless and perfect information is nontrivially valuable. If CONFORM is revealed, the decision maker will surely select ACCEPT, and if NONCONFORM is revealed, REJECT will be selected. The expected utility measure is, therefore,

$$E(U|\text{perfect information}) = .9(2) + .1(1) = 1.9 > 1.4. \tag{5.2}$$

Thus, if the decision maker were risk neutral and if the measures in Exhibit 5.1 were in (say) thousands of dollars we would interpret this as implying our decision maker would pay up to $500 for perfect information in this case.

Now consider a second individual who must decide whether to supply the above decision maker with perfect information. Two options are available: (1) provide no information, or (2) collect and report perfect information. Quite clearly, if the information is *not* provided, the decision maker will select ACCEPT; and if it *is* provided, ACCEPT will be selected if and only if CONFORM is revealed. These acts will be selected (by the decision maker) because they are the decision maker's most preferred choices under the circumstances at hand.

Observe now that the information evaluator—by deciding whether to collect and report the information—can decide which decision rule or strategy the decision maker will employ. Thus the key to analysis of the information evaluator's choices is which decision rule produces the most desirable uncertain set of outcomes *for the evaluator.*

Suppose the evaluator's conditional utility evaluation of the outcomes is as illustrated in Exhibit 5.2.[1]

Exhibit 5.2   Evaluator's conditional outcome evaluations

		Alternative states	
		CONFORM	NONCONFORM
Act choice. by	ACCEPT	5	4
decision maker	REJECT	1	3

Exhibit 5.3 Evaluator's choice problem

| | | Alternative states | |
		CONFORM	NONCONFORM
Choice	Null information	5	4
alternatives	Perfect information	5	3

Combining these evaluations with the anticipated choice behavior of the decision maker provides the choice problem in Exhibit 5.3. Further suppose that the evaluator and decision maker have identical beliefs, or identical probabilities. Then the expected utility *to the evaluator* of not collecting and reporting the information is

$$E(\bar{U}|\text{no information}) = .9(5) + .1(4) = 4.9. \tag{5.3}$$

Similarly, the expected utility of costlessly collecting and reporting perfect information is

$$E(\bar{U}|\text{perfect information}) = .9(5) + .1(3) = 4.8 < 4.9. \tag{5.4}$$

Note that, since the decision maker and evaluator hold identical beliefs, these calculations are identical to those in Eq. (5.1) and Eq. (5.2) except that here we use the evaluator's conditional utility assessments. Moreover, costless perfect information is actually harmful to the evaluator in this case. For example, if the evaluator is risk neutral and if the assessments in Exhibit 5.2 are in (say) thousands of dollars, up to $100 would actually be paid to prevent the decision maker from obtaining such information. The reason is that the decision maker's optimal use of the information is harmful to the evaluator in this case and the implication should be clear: A straightforward application of the single person case, such as Theorem 3, which guarantees you would never pay to suppress costless information, is out of the question at this point.

FORMALIZATION

Let us now formalize the essential aspects of the information evaluation problem illustrated in the preceding section. Since we continue to subscribe to the axioms of choice discussed in Chapter 2, and assume complete specification by the evaluator, formalization entails description of the perceived choice, state, probability, and utility specifications.

Elements of choice

For obvious reasons, we term the evaluator's elements of choice *information systems;* an example would be whether to collect and report some quality attribute in the preceding example. Recognize that, except in the trivial case, the evaluator selects a system that produces signals that will be transmitted to the decision maker; not the signals themselves. In the previous example, it was decided whether to collect and report perfect information, but not which specific state to report. (More will be said about this later.) Let $\eta \in H$ denote a particular information system and $y \in Y$ a particular signal produced by the system. H is then the set of available information systems perceived by the evaluator, and Y is the set of signals that may be produced.

States

We assume that the decision maker and the evaluator share the same specification of possible states. Adopting our previous notation, then, S is the set of mutually exclusive and exhaustive states and $s \in S$ is one such state. Note that by selecting S as the finer (or more "inclusive") description of state necessary for the evaluator and decision maker, we do not sacrifice any generality in adopting the same state specification for both persons.[2]

Utility

The evaluator's utility is assumed to depend on the act selected by the decision maker and the state that actually does occur. Suppose that the evaluator and decision maker perceive the same set of act choices open to the decision maker. Then A is the set of choices available to the decision maker and $a \in A$ is one such choice. In addition, the information system selected by the evaluator, $\eta \in H$, is assumed to be costly and will therefore also affect the evaluator's utility assessment. Denote the evaluator's utility assessment $\bar{U}(s,a,\eta)$. You should interpret this as the evaluator's utility assessment of the cash flow outcome that will occur if information system $\eta \in H$ is selected and state $s \in S$ obtains in conjunction with choice of act $a \in A$ by the decision maker.

Probabilities

The only selected element in the evaluator's utility specification is the information system itself. Hence the evaluator must specify consistent likelihood judgments concerning Nature's state, the system's signal, and the decision maker's act based on that signal. Let $\tilde{\phi}(s)$ denote the probability that state $s \in S$ will obtain. As in Chapter 3, we continue to assume the states are defined so that each information system partitions or classifies the states in S via $y = \eta(s)$. We therefore have signal probabilities of

$$\tilde{\phi}(y|\eta) = \sum_{\substack{s \in S \\ \text{such that} \\ y = \eta(s)}} \tilde{\phi}(s) \tag{5.5}$$

and conditional probabilities of

$$\tilde{\phi}(s|y,\eta) = \begin{cases} \dfrac{\tilde{\phi}(s)}{\tilde{\phi}(y|\eta)} & \text{if } y = \eta(s) \\ 0 & \text{otherwise} \end{cases} \tag{5.6}$$

Finally, the act that the decision maker will select upon receiving signal $y \in Y$ from system $\eta \in H$ must also be specified. In the previous example, the evaluator knew what the decision maker's conditional choice of act was going to be, but this is a limiting special case. Hence we denote the evaluator's perception of the decision maker's choice behavior by $\tilde{\phi}(a|y,\eta)$. This is the probability (perceived by the evaluator) that the decision maker will select act $a \in A$, given that the decision maker has received signal $y \in Y$ from system $\eta \in H$.

Optimization

With such specification, the evaluator will locate the preferred system by selecting the one with the maximum expected utility. We therefore have the following characterization:[3]

$$E(\tilde{U}|a,y,\eta) = \sum_{s \in S} \tilde{U}(s,a,\eta)\, \tilde{\phi}(s|y,\eta) \tag{5.7a}$$

$$E(\tilde{U}|\eta) = \sum_{y \in Y} \tilde{\phi}(y|\eta) \sum_{a \in A} \tilde{\phi}(a|y,\eta)\, E(\tilde{U}|a,y,\eta) \tag{5.7b}$$

and

$$E(\tilde{U}|\eta^*) = \max_{\eta \in H} E(\tilde{U}|\eta). \tag{5.7c}$$

Exhibit 5.4 Information evaluation process

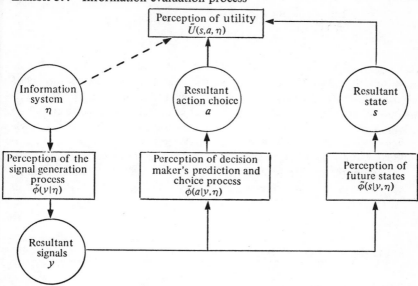

Exhibit 5.4 depicts the entire evaluation process, moving from system specification $\eta \in H$, to signal generation, $y \in Y$, to choice by the decision maker, $a \in A$, and state occurrence, $s \in S$, to utility $\bar{U}(s,a,\eta)$. The evaluator must predict the relationships among the various elements: the signal-generation process, $\tilde{\phi}(y|\eta)$, the decision maker's choice process, $\tilde{\phi}(a|y,\eta)$, and the state occurrences, $\tilde{\phi}(s|y,\eta)$.

We could offer many variants of the basic model in Eq. (5.7), such as separation of the evaluation measure into cost and value components. Although these variations are not essential to our basic development, one of them is interesting enough to warrant a slight digression. This variation concerns the evaluator's knowledge of the decision maker's model.

The special case of a known model

Suppose the evaluator knows the decision maker's model and that for each possible circumstance the optimal act is unique. Under these conditions, $\tilde{\phi}(a|y,\eta)$ becomes degenerate and can be replaced by a decision rule or strategy, say $a = m(y,\eta)$. Let $E(\tilde{U}|m,\eta)$ be the evaluator's expected utility measure in this case:

$$E(\tilde{U}|m,\eta) = \sum_{y \in Y} \tilde{\phi}(y|\eta) \, E(\tilde{U}|m(y,\eta),y,\eta). \qquad (5.8)$$

The interesting question here is: What does explicit knowledge of the decision maker's model contribute to the evaluator's analysis? Simply stated, when the evaluator knows the model used by the decision maker, this reduces one source of uncertainty—uncertainty as to act choice—in the analysis. And, in the limiting case in which knowledge of the model leads to a functional specification, $m(y,\eta)$, it completely eliminates the uncertainty as to act choice. But it does not indicate the information system that should be selected. This remains dependent on his preferences and likelihood judgments, as depicted in Eq. (5.8).[4]

EXAMPLE

Our original example of information system analysis at the beginning of this chapter concerned a situation in which the decision maker and the evaluator held identical probability assessments but divergent tastes. In this example we shall reverse this and postulate divergent probability assessments but identical tastes (except that here we assume the evaluator will also recognize differing cost consequences associated with different information systems).

Suppose a decision maker in a two-product firm faces a problem of determining an optimal schedule for aggregate output. The decision maker is risk neutral and seeks to maximize the firm's expected cash flow. Let a_1 and a_2 denote the output quantities of the two products and p_1 and p_2 their respective uncertain prices. Total revenue is $p_1 a_1 + p_2 a_2$ and total cost is assumed to be $\frac{1}{2}(a_1^2 + a_2^2 + a_1 a_2)$. The decision maker's choice problem is therefore given by

$$\begin{aligned} E(U|a^*) &= \max_{a_1, a_2} E[p_1 a_1 + p_2 a_2 - \tfrac{1}{2}(a_1^2 + a_2^2 + a_1 a_2)] \\ &= \max_{a_1, a_2} a_1 E(p_1) + a_2 E(p_2) - \tfrac{1}{2}(a_1^2 + a_2^2 + a_1 a_2). \end{aligned} \qquad (5.9)$$

The choice of optimal output schedule, a_1 and a_2, is perceived to be completely independent of any effects other than those in Eq. (5.9), and, in particular, no inventory effects are involved. Otherwise, a multiperiod statement of the utility measure would be required. Dif-

Example   71

ferentiation of (5.9) produces the following first-order maximization conditions:[5]

$$\frac{\partial E(U|a)}{\partial a_1} = 0 = E(p_1) - a_1 - \frac{1}{2}a_2,$$

$$\frac{\partial E(U|a)}{\partial a_2} = 0 = E(p_2) - a_2 - \frac{1}{2}a_1,$$ (5.10)

which simplify to

$$a_1^* = \frac{2}{3}(2E(p_1) - E(p_2)),$$

$$a_2^* = \frac{2}{3}(2E(p_2) - E(p_1)).$$ (5.10a)

The state specification consists of various combinations of current prices and the prices that will prevail during the time the output schedule is implemented. Either price in either period can be \$30 or \$60, implying the sixteen possible combinations or states displayed in Exhibit 5.5. (This elaborate state description allows us to examine information systems that will report individual or aggregate current prices.)

Exhibit 5.5 State specifications and probabilities

State	Current price		Future price		Decision maker probabilities	Evaluator probabilities
	$\hat{p}_1$	$\hat{p}_2$	p_1	p_2		
s_1	30	30	30	30	1/64	1/16
s_2	30	30	30	60	3/64	1/16
s_3	30	30	60	30	1/64	1/16
s_4	30	30	60	60	3/64	1/16
s_5	30	60	30	30	0	1/16
s_6	30	60	30	60	1/16	1/16
s_7	30	60	60	30	0	1/16
s_8	30	60	60	60	1/16	1/16
s_9	60	30	30	30	0	0
s_{10}	60	30	30	60	0	0
s_{11}	60	30	60	30	3/32	1/8
s_{12}	60	30	60	60	9/32	1/8
s_{13}	60	60	30	30	0	0
s_{14}	60	60	30	60	0	0
s_{15}	60	60	60	30	0	1/8
s_{16}	60	60	60	60	3/8	1/8

The decision maker's probability assessments are displayed in Exhibit 5.5. (An equivalent expression, focusing on future prices, is displayed in Exhibit 5.6.) Future price expectations, in the absence of additional information, are determined by[6]

$$E(p_1) = 30(\tfrac{1}{8}) + 60(\tfrac{7}{8}) = 56.25$$

and

$$E(p_2) = 30(\tfrac{1}{8}) + 60(\tfrac{7}{8}) = 56.25 \tag{5.11}$$

and the optimal production schedule would be

$$a_1^* = \tfrac{2}{3}(2(56.25) - 56.25) = 37.5$$

and

$$a_2^* = \tfrac{2}{3}(2(56.25) - 56.25) = 37.5, \tag{5.12}$$

with an expected utility to the decision maker of $E(U|a^*) = 2109.375$.

Now suppose that an information evaluator is trying to decide whether to assess and transmit to this decision maker the current prices of the products. Three alternative systems will be considered: (1) report nothing, (2) report the actual current price for each product, or (3) report the sum of the actual current prices. We can interpret this as an accountant trying to decide whether to report price variances in total, report them by individual product, or not report them at all. The evaluator perceives the utility measure in Eq. (5.9), but also recognizes an information system cost of γ_2 for the individual price sys-

Exhibit 5.6 Decision maker's price probabilities

	Product 1		Product 2	
	$p_1 = 30$	$p_1 = 60$	$p_2 = 30$	$p_2 = 60$
Current price probability	$\tfrac{1}{4}$	$\tfrac{3}{4}$	$\tfrac{1}{2}$	$\tfrac{1}{2}$
Future price probability given current price of				
$\hat{p} = 30$	$\tfrac{1}{2}$	$\tfrac{1}{2}$	$\tfrac{1}{4}$	$\tfrac{3}{4}$
$\hat{p} = 60$	0	1	0	1

Example   73

tem and γ_3 for the summed price system. (The cost of the null system—no report—is considered to be zero.) In addition, the evaluator knows the decision maker's probabilities in Exhibit 5.5 and the decision rule in Eq. (5.10a). Finally, the evaluator perceives the price probabilities given in Exhibit 5.5 (and equivalently expressed in Exhibit 5.7).

The evaluator therefore perceives the following price expectations for the future period:

$$E(p_1) = \tfrac{1}{4}(30) + \tfrac{3}{4}(60) = 52.5$$

and

$$E(p_2) = \tfrac{1}{2}(30) + \tfrac{1}{2}(60) = 45. \tag{5.13}$$

And, since the evaluator knows that the decision maker will, in the absence of information on current prices, implement a schedule of $a_1^* = a_2^* = 37.5$, the evaluator's expected utility, if the null system is used, is given by

$$\begin{aligned} E(\tilde{U}|\text{null system}) &= 37.5(52.5) + \\ &\quad 37.5(45) - \tfrac{1}{2}((37.5)^2 + (37.5)^2 + (37.5)^2) \\ &= 1546.875. \end{aligned} \tag{5.14}$$

Now consider the individual current price system. One possible signal is that both current prices are 30, which the evaluator perceives will occur with probability $\tfrac{1}{4}$. If the decision maker knows that the

Exhibit 5.7 Evaluator's price probabilities

	Product 1		Product 2	
	$p_1 = 30$	$p_1 = 60$	$p_2 = 30$	$p_2 = 60$
Current price probability	½	½	½	½
Future price probability given current price of				
$\hat{p} = 30$	½	½	½	½
$\hat{p} = 60$	0	1	½	½

current prices of both products are 30, the following conditional future price expectations will be computed:

$$E(p_1| \hat{p}_1 = \hat{p}_2 = 30) = 30(\tfrac{1}{2}) + 60(\tfrac{1}{2}) = 45$$

and

$$E(p_2| \hat{p}_1 = \hat{p}_2 = 30) = 30(\tfrac{1}{4}) + 60(\tfrac{3}{4}) = 52.5, \tag{5.15}$$

and, using Eq. (5.10a), a future output schedule of $a_1^* = 25$ and $a_2^* = 40$ will be implemented. The evaluator, however, will compute the following conditional future price expectations:

$$E(p_1| \hat{p}_1 = \hat{p}_2 = 30) = 30(\tfrac{1}{2}) + 60(\tfrac{1}{2}) = 45$$

and

$$E(p_2| \hat{p}_1 = \hat{p}_2 = 30) = 30(\tfrac{1}{2}) + 60(\tfrac{1}{2}) = 45, \tag{5.16}$$

and will thus calculate the following conditional expected utility, given the price expectations and the decision maker's choice:

$$E\bar{U}| \hat{p}_1 = \hat{p}_2 = 30) = 25(45) + 40(45) - \tfrac{1}{2}((25)^2 + (40)^2 + (25)(40))$$
$$= 1312.5. \tag{5.17}$$

Exhibit 5.8 shows the calculations for the four possible combinations of signals. Each conditional utility is now weighted by its respective signal probability, and the evaluator's expected utility for individual price reporting is

$$E(\bar{U}|\text{individual price reporting}) = \tfrac{1}{4}(1312.5) + \tfrac{1}{4}(1200.0) +$$
$$\tfrac{1}{4}(1912.5) + \tfrac{1}{4}(1800.0) - \gamma_2$$
$$= 1556.250 - \gamma_2. \tag{5.18}$$

The case for total reporting is similar, except that only three signals are possible. Exhibit 5.8 shows the calculations: here we see that

$$E(\bar{U}|\text{summed reporting}) = 1562.110 - \gamma_3.$$

Thus the evaluator's alternative choices and respective utility evaluations are 1546.875 with the null system. $1556.250 - \gamma_2$ with the individual-reporting system, and $1562.110 - \gamma_3$ with the summed or total reporting system.

Exhibit 5.8 Evaluators utility calculations

System	Signal	Evaluator's signal probability	Decision maker's conditonal price expectations $E(p_1|y)$	$E(p_2|y)$	Decision maker's conditional action choice a_1^*	a_2^*	Evaluator's conditional price expectations $E(p_1|y)$	$E(p_2|y)$	Evaluator's conditional utility
Null	Null	1	56.25	56.25	37.5	37.5	52.5	45	1546.875
Individual price reporting	$y=(30,30)$	$\bar{\phi}(y|\eta)\overset{!}{=}\frac{1}{4}$	45	52.5	25	40	45	45	1312.500
	(30,60)	¼	45	60	20	50	45	45	1200.000
	(60,30)	¼	60	52.5	45	30	60	45	1912.500
	(60,60)	¼	60	60	40	40	60	45	1800.000
Summed price reporting	(60)	¼	45	52.5	25	40	45	45	1312.500
	(90)	½	56.25	54.375	38.75	35	52.5	45	1567.969
	(120)	¼	60	60	40	40	60	45	1800.000

INFORMATION CHOICE BY THE INFORMATION EVALUATOR

The central theme we have been emphasizing in this chapter is that the problem of choice of an information system is fundamentally one of choice in the face of uncertain consequences. Thus, if one accepts the axiomatic structure outlined in Chapter 2, the techniques of decision theory are applicable. The only added development is a separation of tasks between the decision maker and the information evaluator. This separation process carries with it the possibility of divergent assessments of probability and preference.

One aspect of decision analysis explored in Chapter 3 was the value of perfect information calculation. Recall that this datum bounds the improvement in the expected utility measure that is feasible through the introduction of information. And if the decision maker is risk neutral, it can be directly interpreted as the maximum amount our decision maker would pay to acquire perfect information.

The parallel calculation for the information evaluator is quite interesting. In particular, we must address state and decision maker uncertainty. The most obvious way to proceed is to consider costless state revelation in conjunction with allowing the evaluator to select the act. This eliminates state uncertainty and also guarantees optimal choice of $a \in A$ from the evaluator's point of view. Let $\bar{\eta}$ be a null and presumably costless system. We then have[7]

$$\sum_{s \in S} \tilde{\phi}(s) \left\{ \max_{a \in A} \tilde{U}(s,a,\bar{\eta}) \right\} - E(\tilde{U}|\eta^*) \tag{5.19}$$

where, recall, $E(\tilde{U}|\eta^*)$ is the evaluator's maximum expected utility determined in Eq. (5.7).

The measure in Eq. (5.19) bounds the improvement available to the evaluator. If the evaluator is risk neutral, it is the maximum amount that would be paid to learn the state *and* pick the act. Nothing could be better. Hence, it is an upper bound to what the evaluator would pay to learn the state, to identify the decision maker's model, or to control the decision maker's choice.

Another consideration here concerns the general ranking of costless information systems in a complete analysis, as in the subpartitioning result of Theorem 3 for the decision maker. Clearly, as indicated by the example in Exhibit 5.1, this result *does not* extend to the evaluator's ranking of information supplied to and used by the decision maker. But it *does* apply to (private) information supplied to and used by the evaluator. All we need do to gain this interpretation is to interpret the acts in Theorem 3 as information systems.[8]

In sum, complete analysis of the evaluator's problem naturally gives rise to the question of acquiring information before selecting an information system. We are able to then develop an extended value of perfect information expression and to apply the more is better than less (if costless) subpartitioning result.

SIMPLIFICATION OF THE EVALUATOR'S ANALYSIS

Continuing with our idea of recognizing the choice factor in the evaluator's task, we should also recognize that introducing the cost of analysis, as discussed in Chapter 4, will probably cause the evaluator to adopt a simplified analysis. Simplifying the evaluator's analysis usually leads to separating the utility evaluation into two components: benefit and cost. The evaluator, like the decision maker, avoids detailed state-act specifications, expressing the benefit (or value) component as a function of the decision maker's decisions, plus a number of parameters. The specific function, decisions, and set of parameters may, of course, differ from those of the decision maker. Also, the evaluator will likely employ a decision-rule specification of the decision maker's choice.

An extreme form of such simplification occurs when information systems are compared in terms of characteristics such as relevance, verifiability, objectivity, and so on.[9] Here the evaluator simplifies to the point of basing the system choice on an analysis that is quite far removed from the decision context at hand.[10] And all that was said before about simplified analysis applies here as well. In particular, we view the simplified analysis as providing information to the evaluator as opposed to a strictly reliable measure of preference. Presumably, the evaluator takes this into account when trying to balance the cost of errors in the evaluation of an information system against savings in the cost of analysis. But the decision maker presumably does this also, and we recognize the need for control on his part. Hence control of the information evaluation process is also an issue. This is, of course, a fact common to all simplified situations.

SUMMARY

Information system analysis is a complex task that can be approached within the formal framework of decision theory. The essential requirement is provision for a separation between the producer and the user of the information. Moreover, the issues of information seeking and simplification by the evaluator assume a natural position in this view.

We should recognize, however, that the story is not quite complete at this juncture. For example, we might interpret the two individuals as strategically making their choices in an attempt to influence each other's behavior. (Thus $\tilde{\phi}(a|y,\eta)$ would be the evaluator's assessment of the decision maker's strategic behavior.) Here the evaluator might then consider strategically falsifying the information that is transmitted to the decision maker.[11] Of course, this would be out of the question if the decision maker were able to observe any such falsification. Similarly, rather than play strategically, the two might cooperate "for the common good." We might further consider altering incentives so that the two are not at odds over information system choices and uses. The cooperative and incentive possibilities are explored in Chapter 6.

FOOTNOTES

1. The two individuals clearly differ in their evaluations here. You might interpret this as two managers having different perceptions of or tastes for firm-derived outcomes. Different perceptions within an organization are not uncommon. If we could assume that all persons within the firm would agree in their decision model specifications, it would not be necessary to make a distinction between the evaluator and the decision maker. But casual observation should be enough to convince you that this is not the case; and to require such agreement would impose choice restrictions beyond those discussed in Chapter 2. Further observe that many decision makers are provided with incentive systems in an attempt to influence their act choices. This is pursued in Chapter 6.
2. See Marschak (1963) and Feltham (1972).
3. An important but subtle point is involved here. The evaluator must select one $\eta \in H$ and this selection is represented by expected utility maximization. In a more elaborate model, we would *simultaneously* represent the evaluator and the decision maker (using techniques of game theory). One possibility is the evaluator might falsify or add noise to the information before transmitting it to the decision maker. Randomization is the way we model such phenomena, yet the model in Eq. (5.7) does not make any of this explicit. (See note 11 at the end of this chapter.)

   Two interpretations are possible. One is that the evaluator engages in no such behavior (because, say, the choice of $\eta \in H$ is observed by the decision maker and falsification is therefore impossible). The other is that any falsification options are explicitly contained in H. Either way, the evaluator seeks to find the personal best $\eta \in H$, given the decision maker's use of the subsequent signal.

4. Note that if the decision maker operates with a simplified model but the evaluator employs a complete model, $\tilde{\phi}(a|y,\eta)$ must reflect the evaluator's perceptions of the decision maker's simplifications. Thus, if receipt of y from η causes the decision maker to implement an infeasible act, the evaluator's prediction of response upon discovery of the infeasibility, as well as the initial infeasible choice, are included in $\tilde{\phi}(a|y,\eta)$. Also, if the decision maker directly selects only some activities (such as production schedules), but implicitly determines others (such as maintenance and purchasing schedules and the decision model or parameter prediction refinements based on the period's feedback), the evaluator's prediction of all these activities is included in $\tilde{\phi}(a|y,\eta)$.

5. Second-order conditions for a maximum require

$$\frac{\partial^2 E(\cdot)}{\partial a_1^2} = -1 < 0; \frac{\partial^2 E(\cdot)}{\partial a_2^2} = -1 < 0;$$

and

$$\frac{\partial^2 E(\cdot)}{\partial a_1^2} \frac{\partial^2 E(\cdot)}{\partial a_2^2} - \left(\frac{\partial^2 E(\cdot)}{\partial a_1 \partial a_2}\right)^2 = 1 - \frac{1}{4} > 0.$$

6. The probability that $p_1 = 30$ is the sum of $\phi(s)$ over states having $p_1 = 30$, or $1/64 + 3/64 + 0 + 1/16 + 0 + 0 + 0 + 0 = 1/8$.

7. This topic of information seeking by the evaluator is discussed at length in Demski (1972).

8. It is, however, important that we interpret this as information that is strictly private to the evaluator. Even knowing that the evaluator was accessing some information source prior to selection of $\eta \in H$, the decision maker might alter $\tilde{\phi}(a|y,\eta)$. This is the subject of game theory. See Ponssard and Zamir (1973), Baiman (1975), Ponssard (1976), and Demski and Feltham (1976).

9. Familiar examples are the AAA's *A Statement of Basic Accounting Theory* (1966), cost allocation criteria as in Horngren (1977) or Dopuch, et al. (1981), and use of the controllability principle in designing responsibility accounting systems.

10. Demski and Feltham (1976) analyze this issue in considerable detail.

11. The following example, due to David Kreps, illustrates this important point. The decision maker will select one act from $\{a_1, a_2, a_3, a_4, a_5\}$ in a two-state setting with the following utility evaluations:

	s_1	s_2
a_1	0	10
a_2	3	8
a_3	5.9	5.9
a_4	8	3
a_5	10	0

The evaluator, however, has the following utility evaluations:

	s_1	s_2
a_1	0	0
a_2	5	5
a_3	1	1
a_4	5	5
a_5	0	0

Also assume the states are equally likely.

The evaluator has the option of costlessly producing perfect information. Quite clearly, without the information the decision maker will select a_3 thereby providing the evaluator with $E(\tilde{U}|\text{null information}) = 1$. With the information, the decision maker will select a_5 in state s_1 and a_1 in state s_2. Hence, $E(\tilde{U}|\text{perfect information}) = 0$. Also note that $E(U|\text{null information}) = 5.9$ and $E(U|\text{perfect information}) = 10$.

Now suppose the evaluator is able to transmit false information to the decision maker. One such possibility is to tell the true state with probability .6 and the false state with probability .4. (If state s_1 obtains the evaluator will then acknowledge s_1 with probability .6 and s_2 with probability .4; while if s_2 obtains he will acknowledge s_2 with probability .6 and s_1 with probability .4.) The decision maker in turn can do *no better* when faced with such strategic behavior than to pick a_4 if told state s_1 and a_2 if told state s_2. Moreover, if the decision maker actually behaves in this manner, the evaluator can do no better than randomly falsify in the indicated manner. With such a solution, the respective expected utility measures are $E(\tilde{U}|\text{randomization}) = 5$ for the evaluator and $E(U|\text{randomization}) = 6$ for the decision maker!

Chapter Six

A CLOSER LOOK AT SEPARATION

A major difficulty with the evaluator-decision maker analysis in Chapter 5 is that the distinction, while surely descriptive, lacks rationalization. Rather than being in a potential conflict situation, why not model the problem in terms of maximizing the combined good or welfare of the interested parties? Similarly, assessing $\tilde{\phi}(a|y,\eta)$ is qualitatively different from assessing $\tilde{\phi}(s)$ in the sense that the former deals with events subject to control by a second (and possibly reactive or strategic) individual while the latter is more closely associated with events outside of anyone's control. A natural question, then, is why not expand the model to endogenously rather than exogenously specify $\tilde{\phi}(a|y,\eta)$? Finally, accounting information in the firm is often associated with motivating decision makers rather than merely informing them (and thereby revising their state probability assessments). Is it possible, therefore, to broaden our analysis to motivation uses of information?

The purpose of this chapter is to explore these questions, thereby extending and deepening our study of information. We first examine the question of a group utility measure (as opposed to set of individual utility measures) and its maximization. We then examine a model in which one individual hires another and produces information for performance evaluation purposes.

A GROUP UTILITY MEASURE

Return to our original evaluator-decision maker example in Exhibit 5.1. Interpreting each individual as risk neutral and the utility assessments as thousands of dollars, we calculated that the evaluator would actually pay $100 to prevent the decision maker from acquiring perfect information. At the same time, the decision maker would pay up to $500 for perfect information. An obvious solution, therefore, is to transfer $100 from the decision maker to the evaluator and have the costless and perfect information produced. Rather than not cooperating, in other words, we envision them as cooperating (and even making transfer payments) in the choice of an information system.[1]

Now observe that the payment from the decision maker to the evaluator could be anywhere between $100 and $500. At $100, only the decision maker benefits, and at $500 only the evaluator benefits. All other schemes split the overall gain. So to fully solve the information system choice problem we should address (1) what system should be selected, (2) what transfers (if any) among the participants should be made, and (3) how the information subsequently produced should be used. You will notice that each of these questions was answered in one particular way in Chapter 5.

Rather than confront these questions directly, suppose we ask instead whether we can find a group utility measure whose maximization will produce the desired (system, transfer, and use) choices. What properties should such a group utility measure have? Four properties will be offered. To make certain the question is interesting, we will focus on a general case of at least two individuals and at least three alternatives.

First, the group utility scheme should always work: No matter what the utility assessments of the individuals, we ought to be able to construct a complete and transitive ranking of the available alternatives so as to provide a group utility measure. This is typically referred to as a *universal domain* condition.[2] It is a reasonable condition to impose in the sense that all individuals are assumed to have complete and transitive rankings (recall our representation discussion in Chapter 2) and we ask no more of the group assessment. Beyond this we place no restrictions whatever on the choice setting or the individuals. Weird tastes are perfectly acceptable, as long as they are consistent in the sense of being complete and transitive. Similarly, the choice setting might involve cash outcomes, as we have generally assumed for expositional reasons, or a myriad of outcomes such as cash today, cash tomorrow, prestige, friendship, and leisure. But you should also recognize that the universal domain requirement is not exactly trivial. A straightforward majority rule voting procedure will produce intransitivities. See the case of three individuals, three information systems, and the particular utility assessments in Exhibit 6.1. Simple majority rule ranks η_1 above η_2, η_2 above η_3, and η_3 above η_1!

Exhibit 6.1   Intransitive voting illustration

| | | *Individual expected utility assessments* | | |
		$i = 1$	$i = 2$	$i = 3$
Information	η_1	3	1	2
system	η_2	2	3	1
	η_3	1	2	3

Second, the group utility assessment across two alternatives must be such that if each individual strictly prefers the first to the second alternative, then the group assessment must strictly prefer the first to the second. This condition is termed *Pareto optimality*. If Pareto optimality ever failed, we would be offering a theory of group behavior based upon the individuals acting so as to systematically deny themselves what they want. Also notice that in our simple example where only the expected cash flow is important and where cash transfer payments are allowed, this condition guarantees that the information will be produced. Universal domain, in turn, ensures that our procedure will in fact work on this (as well as every other) problem. The remaining two conditions, when applied to the example, are designed to place conditions on the precise identification of the transfer payment.

Third, the group utility assessment is based only on the individuals' rankings of the available alternatives. Suppose we are selecting between η_1 and η_2 and for a particular set of individual utility assessments we arrive at a group assessment that η_1 is ranked above η_2. Now consider any other individual assessments that are the same for η_1 and η_2, but unconstrained otherwise. Then our procedure applied to these new assessments must also rank η_1 over η_2. The idea is that assessments of unavailable or "irrelevant" alternatives are *not* to be used by the procedure. We base the group assessments on rankings but not on "intensity" of preference. The reason is straightforward. We want to rule out interpersonal utility comparisons in the procedure, simply because the uniqueness of the utility measurement (again recall Chapter 2) makes such a notion meaningless. This condition is termed *independence of irrelevant alternatives.*

Finally, we disallow dictators in our group assessment procedure. There cannot exist an individual who, regardless of personal assessments and regardless of everyone else's assessments, is always so influential that the group always prefers what he or she prefers.

The difficulty, now, is that *no* group utility assessment exists that will satisfy these relatively innocuous requirements. This disconcerting result is due to Arrow (1963).[3]

Theorem 4:   Universal domain, Pareto optimality, independence of irrelevant alternatives, and nondictatorship are mutually inconsistent requirements to impose on a group utility assessment.

Thus whatever the group does, however the evaluator-decision maker setting is modeled, we violate at least one of the four conditions. More important, this is the reason we have not offered a model based on a group preference measure. Requiring even modest standards of assessment, the fancied group measure does not exist. We therefore cannot, admitting to these standards, describe the problem as though the individuals resolved their conflicts so as to maximize some group utility measure. The measure does not exist.[4]

Judicious retreat is called for, and we now turn to a highly specialized subset of the class of evaluation-decision maker settings.

THE PRINCIPAL-AGENT MODEL

Return, then, to our focus on the evaluator. The determinants of outcome are the choice of information system, Nature's choice of state, and the decision maker's choice of act upon receipt of the eventual signal. The formulation in Chapter 5 assumed specification of the decision maker's choice behavior with a probability function, $\tilde{\phi}(a|y,\eta)$. Here we examine a setting in which the decision maker (or agent) is hired by the evaluator (or principal) to select and implement act $a \in A$. The decision maker (or agent) is paid for services and the evaluator (or principal) enjoys the outcome less the amount paid to the decision maker (or agent). Examples are abundant: owners and managers, parents and elementary school teachers, patients and physicians, clients and lawyers, and so on.

The literature refers to this as the principal-agent model; and we will do likewise so as to distinguish it as a special case of the more general model in Chapter 5.[5]

Example

Consider a setting in which three acts, three states, and the cash flow outcomes displayed in Exhibit 6.2 are present. The states are equally likely. The principal is risk neutral and therefore evaluates options in terms of the expected value of the cash flow that will be eventually received. The catch here is that the act is some type of productive "ef-

Exhibit 6.2 Conditional cash flows

		States		
		s_1	s_2	s_3
	$a = 5$	\$42000	\$42000	\$18000
Acts	$a = 3$	\$18000	\$42000	\$18000
	$a = 0$	\$0	\$0	\$0

fort'' that must be supplied by a second individual or agent. This agent, in turn, experiences pecuniary and nonpecuniary returns from employment, enjoying receiving cash and not enjoying supplying effort. The agent's utility for cash z and effort a is

$$U(z,a) = \sqrt{z} - a^2. \qquad (6.1)$$

Note in particular that the agent is risk and effort averse.

The problem, of course, is to motivate the agent to supply effort in exchange for cash. Exactly how this is done depends on what the principal and agent *jointly* know or observe. They cannot contract on effort if the principal does not observe the effort. The agent, in such a setting, might be able to shirk on supplying effort. Would you play roulette over the telephone? (If so, send a retainer and call me at any hour!)

Suppose both parties know the cash outcome, actual state, and actual effort after the fact. Then the agent's payment can depend on the cash outcome, state, and effort. Remember, however, that our principal is risk neutral while the agent is risk averse. Hence, whatever payment arrangement is agreed upon would consist of a constant wage to the agent in exchange for some agreed upon effort supply. A non-constant wage dumps risk on the agent and this doesn't make sense. Risk is a "bad" to the agent while it is a matter of indifference to the principal.

Further suppose the agent is not a slave. Any pay-for-effort arrangement must, then, be sufficiently attractive to keep the agent from seeking alternative employment. Here we assume the arrangement must have an expected utility of at least 100, as perceived by the agent. To implement the $a = 5$ alternative, the principal's problem would be

$$\max_{z \geq 0} \tfrac{1}{3}(42000 - z) + \tfrac{1}{3}(42000 - z) + \tfrac{1}{3}(18000 - z)$$
$$\text{subject to } \sqrt{z} - (5)^2 \geq 100 \qquad (6.2a)$$

which has a fairly obvious solution of $z^* = (125)^2 = \$15,625$ and an expected cash flow to the principal of $18,375.

The analysis for $a = 3$ is

$$\max_{z \geq 0} \tfrac{1}{3}(18000 - z) + \tfrac{1}{3}(42000 - z) + \tfrac{1}{3}(18000 - z)$$
$$\text{subject to } \sqrt{z} - (3)^2 \geq 100 \qquad (6.2b)$$

which implies $z^* = (109)^2 = \$11,881$ with an expected cash flow to the principal of $14,119. The $a = 0$ alternative is clearly inferior and the

$a = 5$, $z^* = \$15,625$ option will be selected. Also note, before continuing, that the nature of the contract here is payment of $15,625 if and only if $a = 5$ is supplied. The agent will not shirk because $a = 3$ or $a = 0$ will be detected for certain, the resulting payment will be nil, and $U(15625,5) > U(0,0) > U(0,3)$.[6]

Now change the story and suppose the principal and agent jointly observe *only* the cash flow. The previously determined contract is now unenforceable. In particular, if offered such a contract the agent could select $a = 3$ and merely claim "bad luck" if the principal complains upon observing an outcome of $18,000. $a = 0$ would not be selected because the resulting outcome would unequivocally identify the agent's shirking. Of course, none of this would concern us if the agent were completely trustworthy.

Without an ability to observe the agent's choice of $a \in A$, and without a completely trustworthy agent, the principal must offer an acceptable contract that has the added feature of making it in the agent's perceived self-interest to supply the desired effort. To see how we do this, let z_{42} be the agent's payment if the $42,000 outcome is observed, z_{18} if $18,000 is observed, and z_0 if $0 is observed. Since both parties observe only the outcome, this and only this type of payment scheme can be constructed on the basis of jointly observed data. Consider, now, a scheme to supply $a = 5$:

$$\max_{z_0, z_{18}, z_{42} \geq 0} \tfrac{1}{3}(42000 - z_{42}) + \tfrac{1}{3}(42000 - z_{42}) + \tfrac{1}{3}(18000 - z_{18})$$

$$\text{subject to } \tfrac{2}{3}\sqrt{z_{42}} + \tfrac{1}{3}\sqrt{z_{18}} - (5)^2 \geq 100$$

$$\tfrac{2}{3}\sqrt{z_{42}} + \tfrac{1}{3}\sqrt{z_{18}} - (5)^2 \geq \tfrac{2}{3}\sqrt{z_{18}} + \tfrac{1}{3}\sqrt{z_{42}} - (3)^2$$

$$\tfrac{2}{3}\sqrt{z_{42}} + \tfrac{1}{3}\sqrt{z_{18}} - (5)^2 \geq \sqrt{z_0} - (0)^2. \tag{6.3}$$

The first constraint guarantees that the package offers the agent an expected utility of at least 100; otherwise the employment offer will not be accepted. The second guarantees that $a = 5$ is perceived as being at least as desirable to the agent as $a = 3$, and the third does the same for $a = 0$. A solution is readily found with $z_0 = \$0$, $z_{18} = \$8,649$, and $z_{42} = \$19,881$. The principal's expected cash flow is $17,863.[7] This, along with parallel details for $a = 3$ and $a = 0$ is summarized in Exhibit 6.3.

Several comments are in order here. First, the principal will offer the contract with $z_0 = \$0$, $z_{18} = \$8,649$, and $z_{42} = \$19,881$ which supports an effort supply of $a = 5$ and provides an expected cash flow to the principal of $17,863. Strictly speaking, this solution has the agent

Exhibit 6.3 Incentive arrangements when only cash outcome is jointly observed

Self enforcing effort supply	Incentive payments			Agent expected utility			Principal expected utility		
	z_0	z_{18}	z_{42}	$a = 0$	$a = 3$	$a = 5$	$a = 0$	$a = 3$	$a = 5$
$a = 5$	$0	$8649	$19881	0 .	100	100	0	13607	17863
$a = 3$	$0	$11881	$11881	0	100	84	0	14119	22119
$a = 0^*$	$10000	$0	$0	100	− 9	− 25	− 10000	26000	34000

*Another way to interpret the $a = 0$ case is to observe that it is substantially cheaper not to hire the agent than to hire and pay the agent to do nothing. Here, however, we are examining contracts that force a particular a while observing the constraint on expected utility of at least 100.

indifferent between $a = 3$ and $a = 5$. We assume that when faced with multiple optima, the agent selects from among his best acts according to the principal's desires. Hence, with agent indifference between $a = 3$ and $a = 5$ in this contracting arrangement, we assume $a = 5$ will be chosen because the principal prefers $a = 5$ to $a = 3$. (If this is not the case, use of $z_{42} = \$19,881.01$ will do the trick.)

Second, the interpretation is important and straightforward. The principal would prefer to offer $z_{18} = z_{42} = \$15,625$. The agent is indifferent between the two, but the latter is *not* self-enforcing here. The constant wage *insures* the agent against the cash flow variation; this is desirable because the agent is risk averse while the principal is risk neutral. But such an insurance scheme makes it in the agent's self-interest to shirk in supplying effort. (This phenomenon is called *moral hazard*.) To control for the lack of incentive to supply $a = 5$, the principal uses an incentive arrangement that dumps some risk on the agent. The principal has no better choice in the absence of additional information. Third, as alluded to previously, we interpret this payment scheme as an incentive arrangement. The agent receives a payment of $8649 plus a bonus of $19,881 − \$8,649 = \$11,232$ if the actual cash flow is $42,000. The incentive scheme is not particularly desirable on risk sharing grounds, but it does entice the agent to supply the desired effort. Typical franchise arrangements, managerial incentive schemes, contingent legal fees, and cost-plus contracting provide ready examples of such phenomena. Fourth, and finally, the principal would pay up to $18,375 − \$17,863 = \$512$ to (directly or indirectly) identify the agent's act in this case.

Formalization

Before introducing information considerations, it is probably best to offer a more formal statement of the problem we are dealing with. We assume the principal is risk neutral and seeks to maximize his or her expected cash flow. The agent has utility for cash and disutility for acts or effort. The agent's particular utility function for cash flow z and effort a is given by

$$U(z,a) = F(z) - V(a) \qquad (6.4)$$

and the expected value of $U(z,a)$ must be at least $\bar{U}$ to make the employment offer attractive. Both individuals assess identical state probabilities, denoted $\phi(s)$. The total cash flow under state $s \in S$ and act $a \in A$ is denoted by $x = f(s,a)$. Incentive arrangements are confined to payments based on this cash flow. Though superior arrangements based on state or effort contracting may be available they are infeasible here because the principal and the agent jointly observe only the cash flow. We denote the payment to the agent if $x = f(s,a)$ is observed by $z = z(x)$. Thus, if total cash flow x is observed, the agent is paid $z(x)$ and the principal receives $x - z(x)$. The principal's problem is now formulated as[8]

$$\max_{\substack{a \in A \\ z(x) \geq \bar{z}}} \sum_{s \in S} [f(s,a) - z(f(s,a))]\, \phi(s)$$

$$\text{subject to } \sum_{s \in S} F(z(f(\cdot)))\phi(s) - V(a) \geq \bar{U}$$

$$a \in \operatorname{argmax} \sum_{s \in S} F(z(f(\cdot)))\phi(s) - V(a) \qquad (6.5)$$

(where $\bar{z}$ is a minimum feasible payment).

The formulation, that is, seeks a self-enforcing effort supply and payment schedule that maximizes the principal's expected utility. The first constraint makes certain the arrangement is attractive to the agent. The second constraint is the self-enforcing property; the argmax $h(\cdot)$ notation denotes the set of arguments that maximize the function $h(\cdot)$; and

$$a \in \operatorname{argmax} \sum_{s \in S} F(z(f(s,a))) - V(a)$$

simply means that the singled-out effort supply is optimal from the agent's perspective. Moreover, the maximization over $a \in A$ reflects the assumption that if alternate optima exist for the agent, the agent-optimal act most preferred by the principal is chosen.

From the principal's point of view, then, the agent's behavior is treated as endogenous in the analysis. Returning to the example with

$$z_0 = z(0) = 0, \quad z_{18} = z(18000) = \$8,649,$$

and

$$z_{42} = z(42000) = \$19,881,$$

the principal determines $\tilde{\phi}(a = 5|z(\cdot)) = 1$. We have, in other words, constructed a setting in which the evaluator's assessment of the decision maker's choice is a product of rather than an input to the analysis.

INFORMATION QUESTIONS

Two types of information questions now emerge. One concerns production and use of information by the agent to improve the quality of the effort supply decision. We have, in fact, discussed this type of problem at length in Chapters 3 and 5. The only added dimension is that the incentive structure will likely now be sensitive to the agent's information, even if the principal does not personally observe the information. The other information question concerns production and use of information by the parties so as to improve their contracting arrangement. Again the ultimate concern is the improvement of the quality of the effort selection (or risk sharing); but it is important to realize that such information may actually be produced *after* $a \in A$ is selected. Since the former has already been extensively discussed, we will offer a short example to illustrate its inclusion within the principal-agent model, and then turn to information that is designed to improve contracting arrangements.

Example

Return to our original example in Exhibit 6.2 but now assume the agent will costlessly learn the state before selecting the effort or act. The principal will not observe the state but does know that the agent will.

Quite clearly, the best way to use this information is to select $a = 5$ if state s_1 is revealed and to select $a = 3$ in the other two cases.

The agent's payment, however, can only depend on the cash outcome; and we therefore determine the optimal contract arrangement from

$$\max_{z_{18},z_{42} \geq 0} \quad \tfrac{1}{3}(42000 - z_{42}) + \tfrac{1}{3}(42000 - z_{42}) + \tfrac{1}{3}(18000 - z_{18})$$

$$\text{subject to} \quad \tfrac{1}{3}(\sqrt{z_{42}} - (5)^2) + \tfrac{1}{3}(\sqrt{z_{42}} - (3)^2) +$$

$$\tfrac{1}{3}(\sqrt{z_{18}} - (3)^2) \geq 100$$

$$\sqrt{z_{42}} - (5)^2 \geq \sqrt{z_{18}} - (3)^2$$

$$\sqrt{z_{42}} - (3)^2 \geq \sqrt{z_{42}} - (5)^2$$

$$\sqrt{z_{18}} - (3)^2 \geq \sqrt{z_{18}} - (5)^2. \qquad (6.6)$$

The first constraint again ensures an expected utility to the agent of at least 100. The second forces selection of $a = 5$ over $a = 3$ if s_1 is observed and the last two force selection of $a = 3$ over $a = 5$ if s_2 or s_3 are observed. We should also make certain $a = 0$ is not selected, but setting $z_0 = 0$ will accomplish this here. Of course, only the first two constraints are binding and we readily find $z_{18} = \$10746.78$ and $z_{42} = \$14320.11$ with an expected cash flow to the principal of $\$20,871$.[9]

Further notice that the contract in the first example (with $z_{18} = \$8,649$ and $z_{42} = \$19,881$) will entice the agent to use the information in exactly this manner here, but is much more expensive to the principal. (Why?) The point is that the optimal contracting arrangement will be sensitive to the information that is being made available to the agent.

Indeed another way to see this is to inquire whether the principal should arrange to have the agent (but *not* the principal) acquire costless and perfect information. Treating this as an evaluator-decision maker problem, we have the $\tilde{U}(s,a,\eta)$ data displayed in Exhibit 6.4. Combining this with the displayed $\tilde{\phi}(a|y,\eta)$ assessments, we see that the evaluator prefers to have the information supplied to the decision maker in this case:

$$E(\tilde{U}|\text{no information}) = \tfrac{1}{3}(22119) + \tfrac{1}{3}(22119) + \tfrac{1}{3}(9351) = 17863$$

and

$$E(\tilde{U}|\text{perfect information}) = \tfrac{1}{3}(27679.89) + \tfrac{1}{3}(27679.89)$$

$$+ \tfrac{1}{3}(7253.22) = 20871. \qquad (6.7)$$

Exhibit 6.4   Evaluator-decision maker interpretation

No information case

	$\bar{U}(\cdot)$ assessments			$\tilde{\phi}(a\|\cdot)$ assessments
	s_1	s_2	s_3	
$a = 5$	$22119	$22119	$9351	$\tilde{\phi}(a = 5) = 1$
$a = 3$	$9351	$22119	$9351	
$a = 0$	$0	$0	$0	

Perfect information case

	$\bar{U}(\cdot)$ assessments			$\hat{\phi}(a\|\cdot)$ assessments
	s_1	s_2	s_3	
$a = 5$	$27679.89	$27679.89	$7253.22	$\tilde{\phi}(a = 5\|s_1 \text{ revealed}) = 1$
$a = 3$	$7253.22	$27679.89	$7253.22	$\tilde{\phi}(a = 3\|s_2 \text{ revealed}) = 1$
$a = 0$	$0	$0	$0	$\tilde{\phi}(a = 3\|s_3 \text{ revealed}) = 1$

This example allows us to demonstrate the extension of the evaluator-decision maker model to a setting with endogenous determination of the decision maker's choice behavior.[10]

Performance evaluation

Now consider the production and use of additional information that is to be used to improve the contracting arrangements between the principal and the agent. We may think of this as engaging in some type of performance evaluation. Without any such information, the contracting arrangement is confined to an incentive payment dependent on the jointly observed cash flow datum; while with such information the incentive arrangement may depend on both the cash flow datum and the performance evaluation. Quite clearly, access to any costless performance evaluation can never be harmful to the principal, who always has the option of offering the contract that would be offered without such information.

On the other hand, such information is of quite limited interest if the agent is risk or effort neutral. In the former case, the obvious solution is to sell the agent the firm. The agent then fully internalizes the effects of any shirking and no effort incentive supply problem arises.[11] Similarly, if work neutral (with $V(a) = $ constant), the agent will implement any effort level desired by the principal. (The agent has no incentive to do otherwise.) And we again have no incentive problem.[12]

In either case, then, the performance evaluation would be useless.[13] The optimal contracting arrangement in place, based only on cash flow, cannot be improved upon. This is why we stated the problem in Eq. (6.5) with the agent risk and work averse. Recall, now, that in the original example in Exhibit 6.2 where the agent is risk and effort averse that the principal would pay up to $512 for a performance evaluation measure that would perfectly reveal the agent's act. We explore this further with a series of examples.

Example 1 Consider the original example in Exhibit 6.2, but now suppose a costless performance evaluation system is available. This system will distinguish state s_3 from states s_1 and s_2 at the time the cash flow is observed, but too late to directly affect the choice of act. With such an evaluation, we can envision an incentive payment depending on the observed cash flow and the observed evaluation—$\{s_3\}$ or $\{s_1,s_2\}$. A little reflection, though, should convince you that an optimal contract consists of

$$z = \begin{cases} \$15,625 & \text{if \$42,000 is observed in} \\ & \text{conjunction with } \{s_1,s_2\} \\ & \text{or \$18,000 with } \{s_3\} \\ \\ \$0 & \text{otherwise} \end{cases} \tag{6.8}$$

This will entice the agent to select an effort of $a = 5$, thereby guaranteeing a utility of 100 regardless of the state—the best possible solution in this case.

Note in particular what has transpired here. Without the evaluation, the optimal contract is an incentive arrangement paying a bonus if the $42,000 outcome is observed. With the evaluation, the optimal arrangement is a penalty clause. A budget of $42,000 is again established. $15,625 is paid if the budget is met or if a shortfall in conjunction with state s_3 is observed. In all other cases a penalty is administered (termination?). And the evaluation structure is such that the agent can guarantee, through choice of effort, that the penalty is never administered.

Clearly the principal would pay up to $512 for such an evaluation system. But why? The exact same act is taken with and without the evaluation being available. The source of the gain here is removal of the risky incentive payment. The expected payment to the agent without the evaluation system is higher than $15,625 (it is precisely $\frac{2}{3}(19,881) + \frac{1}{3}(8,649) = \$16,137$) because the incentive payment is risky.

Example 2 A similar set up here is an evaluation system under which the actual state can be discerned, but the decision on whether to produce the evaluation can be deferred until the cash flow itself is observed. One way to utilize this system is to produce the evaluation when a cash flow of $18,000 is observed. A contract paying

$$z = \begin{cases} \$15,625 & \text{if } \$42,000 \text{ is observed} \\ \$15,625 & \text{if } \$18,000 \text{ and } \{s_3\} \text{ are observed} \\ \$0 & \text{otherwise} \end{cases} \tag{6.9}$$

will force selection of $a = 5$. Again we have a budget interpretation, and an "investigation" is called for if the budget of $42,000 is not achieved. Here, however, the decision on whether to produce the evaluation can be deferred. And in this particular scheme the evaluation would be produced (under $a = 5$) with probability $\frac{1}{3}$. Hence our principal would pay up to $3(512) = \$1536$ for such an evaluation scheme, assuming the payment is made only if the investigation is actually called for.

This, in turn, raises an important point.[14] Under this arrangement, the principal is somehow committing to investigate when the budget is not met. Otherwise, it might be reasoned that the agent has already acted and was properly motivated to select $a = 5$; so the cheapest way out is to renege and not investigate. The principal would merely pay the agent the promised $15,625 and save the investigation cost. The flaw is that if this line of reasoning was anticipated, the agent will surely select $a = 3$![15]

Example 3 The idea of conditioning the production of evaluation data on the observed cash flow and of being able to commit to a particular information acquisition strategy raises an additional issue of random sampling. Suppose the evaluation in Example 2 costs $500 if it is ordered. If always ordered when the $18,000 outcome is observed, the contract in Eq. (6.9) provides an expected cash flow to the principal of:

$$\frac{1}{3}(42000 - 15625) + \frac{1}{3}(42000 - 15625) + \frac{1}{3}(18000 - 15625 - 500)$$

$$= 18208.33. \tag{6.10}$$

Suppose, however, that the principal will investigate only with probability .384 if the $18,000 outcome is observed. The contract is

$$z = \begin{cases} \$15,625 & \text{if } \$42,000 \text{ is observed} \\ \$15,625 & \text{if } \$18,000 \text{ is observed and} \\ & \text{no investigation is made} \\ \$15,625 & \text{if } \$18,000 \text{ is observed in} \\ & \text{conjunction with } \{s_3\} \\ \$0 & \text{otherwise} \end{cases} \tag{6.11}$$

Here the agent will select $a = 5$. In particular, under $a = 5$, surely a payment of $15,625 would be received, implying a utility of $\sqrt{15625} - (5)^2 = 100$; but under $a = 3$, the agent faces

$$\tfrac{1}{3}(.384)\sqrt{0} + \tfrac{1}{3}(.616)\sqrt{15625} + \tfrac{2}{3}\sqrt{15625} - (3)^2 = 100 \tag{6.12}$$

because the penalty ($z = 0$) is incurred only if the agent is investigated and found to be producing $18,000 in conjunction with state s_1. (You should contrast this with the case where the investigation will reveal the act rather than the state.)

The principal's lot, now, is considerably improved relative to that of guaranteed investigation when $18,000 is observed:

$$\tfrac{1}{3}(42000 - 15625) + \tfrac{1}{3}(42000 - 15625)$$
$$+ \tfrac{1}{3}(.384)(18000 - 15625 - 500)$$
$$+ \tfrac{1}{3}(.616)(18000 - 15625) = 18311. \tag{6.13}$$

This depends, of course, on the principal being able to make a committment to such a "sampling" scheme. Otherwise the principal is lacking in incentive.[16]

SUMMARY

We see, therefore, that the basic analysis begun in Chapter 5 extends to motivation or incentive issues as well. Here we envision the information as providing an evaluation that is used to structure contracting arrangements. This allows us to treat $\tilde{\phi}(a|y,\eta)$ as being determined in the analysis, rather than as an input to it. And it also allows us to talk about a much broader use of accounting information within the firm. (But accepting the conditions in Theorem 4 we do not go so far as to model this in general as the maximization of some global or group utility assessment.)

Though we never extended the setting to combine the two information uses, a two-period model would readily accomplish this. The information produced at the end of the first period, say first month, might then be useful in evaluating the first month's decision as well as in guiding the second month's decision.[17]

FOOTNOTES

1. Sundem (1979) explores the gains to cooperation in this case, as well as various game theoretic formulations of the evaluator-decision maker set up. Also see our discussion at Eq. (5.19).

2. To understand this terminology, notice that the group's ranking is meant to depend in some way on individual rankings. Let Z be the set of all complete and transitive binary relations on the set of alternatives in question. Each individual $i = 1, \ldots, n$ is then identified by a preference ranking $\gtrsim_i \in Z$. And we seek a function such that the group's ranking, $\gtrsim$, is in Z and is given by $\gtrsim = f(\gtrsim_1, \ldots, \gtrsim_n)$. To always work, or to satisfy the universal domain condition, means that this function is defined over all logical combinations of $\gtrsim_i \in Z, i = 1 \ldots, n$.

3. Indeed, Arrow's result has created an entire subindustry within economics. Luce and Raiffa (1957) provide an excellent introduction. Then see Arrow (1963), Sen (1970), Kelly (1978), and Green and Laffont (1979), in that order.

4. It is possible to construct a group measure in heavily restricted settings. Consider the cash outcome case. If everyone is risk neutral and has homogeneous beliefs, we in effect have a single commodity world—expected cash flow. We are now able (by restricting the individuals' preferences) to provide a group assessment. An example would be maximization of the group's total expected cash flow.

   Indeed we can say much more in this restricted setting of cash flow outcomes. Wilson (1968) provides a setting in which a group of risk averse individuals that makes a joint decision and shares the resulting outcome acts so as to maximize the expected value of a group utility function; and Demski (1973) extends this to questions of information analysis. The price, however, is high. Outcomes are real valued (here interpreted as cash flow) and with heterogeneous beliefs the individuals' risk aversion must be closely aligned.

5. This literature is new and extensive: Spence and Zeckhauser (1971), Mirrlees (1974 and 1976), Ross (1973 and 1974), Stiglitz (1974) Jensen and Meckling (1976), Demski and Feltham (1978), Harris and Raviv (1978), Holmstrom (1979), Shavell (1979), and Demski (1980).

6. The argument for a constant wage in this case is easily formalized. For $a = 5$, the general statement would be

$$\max_{z_1, z_2, z_3 \geq 0} \tfrac{1}{3}(42000 - z_1) + \tfrac{1}{3}(42000 - z_2) + \tfrac{1}{3}(18000 - z_3)$$

$$\text{subject to } \tfrac{1}{3}\sqrt{z_1} + \tfrac{1}{3}\sqrt{z_2} + \tfrac{1}{3}\sqrt{z_3} - (5)^2 \geq 100$$

and the unique solution is $z_1 = z_2 = z_3 = 15625$.

7. To reproduce this solution, set $z_0 = \$0$ and assume the first two constraints are binding. This gives two equations in two unknowns and the identified solution. Then assume either of the first two constraints is not binding. The implied solution violates the identified nonbinding constraint. (And you can increase z_0 up to the point where the third constraint is binding.)

8. Here we assume both individuals know the structure of the problem, have the same beliefs, and jointly observe only the cash flow. Moreover, and as should be clear from our formulation, the principal is assumed to know the agent's utility assessments.

9. Contrast this with the case where both individuals observe the state. Here the same act selections are optimal but the agent has guaranteed utility of 100 in each state (via a payment of $15625 in s_1 and $11,881 otherwise. The principal's expected cash flow is $20871. The two expected cash flows agree only because of rounding error; the principal is slightly better off in this case.

10. An interesting question here concerns whether a result similar to the general ranking in Theorem 3 could be provided. This is a delicate issue, however, because the information is not necessarily used optimally from the principal's point of view. And this allows us to construct counter examples to the general proposition that "more" information supplied to the agent before $a \in A$ is selected is not harmful. Consider the following example with three equally likely states:

	States		
	s_1	s_2	s_3
a_1	$42000	$42000	$18000
a_2	$18000	$42000	$18000
a_3	$18000	$0	$0

The principal is risk neutral while the agent is risk and effort averse with $U(z,a) = \sqrt{z} - V(a)$. Moreover, $V(a_1) = 25$, $V(a_2) = 24$, and $V(a_3) = 0$. We also require $z \geq \$15,129$ unless the cash flow is zero, in which case $z \geq 0$; and the agent's reservation expected utility is 100.

With contracting confined to the jointly observable cash flow, the solution is to use $a = a_1$ with $z(0) = 0$, $z(18000) = \$15,129$, and $z(42000) = \$15,876$. This provides the principal with an expected cash flow of \$18,373.

On the other hand, suppose the agent acquires perfect and costless state information. (This occurs after the contract is signed, is known by the principal, but observed only by the agent.) The best the principal can do is offer $z(0) = \$0$, $z(18000) = \$15,129$, and $z(42000) = \$21,904$. This provides the principal with an expected cash flow of \$14,354.33!

Kwon et al. (1979), Holmstrom (1979), and Shavell (1979) discuss the question of additional information in the principal-agent model.

11. A bankruptcy condition is present here in that selling the firm for a fixed price assumes the agent can make the payment regardless of what state eventually obtains. (Recall the $z(x) \geq \overline{z}$ constraint in Eq. (6.5).)

12. This depends on the principal being risk neutral. Otherwise, the two will always share in the firm's risk in any optimal contracting arrangement. And in this case, even with no effort aversion, the two may disagree over the best $a \in A$ because of differences in risk aversion. This is explored in Wilson (1968, 1969) and Ross (1973, 1974).

13. Indeed, we may interpret risk and effort aversion as necessary conditions for any performance evaluation to be useful in this simple principal-agent model with jointly observed cash flow and a risk neutral principal. On the other hand, these conditions are not sufficient. If the cash flow data in Exhibit 6.2 were changed so that $f(s = s_1, a = 3) = f(s_1, 3) = 17,000$, no incentive problem would exist. Merely pay \$15,625 if $x = \$42,000$ or $x = \$18,000$ is observed and \$0 otherwise. The agent will select $a = 5$ thereby guaranteeing a wage of \$15,625 and a utility of 100. See Demski and Feltham (1978), Harris and Raviv (1978), and Holmstrom (1979) for further discussion of necessary and sufficient conditions for performance evaluation to be useful.

14. A subtle comparison with the typical "when to investigate" literature (surveyed by Kaplan (1975)) also arises here. This literature views the outcome distribution as given and as independent of the investigation policy. Here, however, the outcome distribution is quite dependent on the investigation policy chosen.

15. Rather than a commitment of some sort that is believable to the agent, we could also rely on contracted payments that make it worthwhile to investigate even after the fact. Suppose the investigation costs \$500, if ordered by the principal. A contract paying

$$z = \begin{cases} \$15,625 & \text{if } \$42,000 \text{ is observed} \\ \$15,625 & \text{if } \$18,000 \text{ is observed, an investigation} \\ & \text{is ordered, and } \{s_3\} \text{ is observed} \\ \$40,000 & \text{if } \$18,000 \text{ is observed and no} \\ & \text{investigation is ordered} \\ \$0 & \text{if } \$0 \text{ is observed} \end{cases}$$

will make it in the agent's best interest to select $a = 5$ and the principal's best interest to investigate if \$18,000 is observed.

16. The .384 investigation strategy and contract in Eq. (6.11) are, in fact, the optimal arrangements here when the investigation costs $500 and the principal can commit to any investigation strategy.
17. This is explored in Demski (1980).

Chapter Seven

MARKET CONSIDERATIONS

INFORMATION MARKETS
MARKET ACTS
FOOTNOTES

We have studied how choice behavior that can be represented by expected utility maximization provides a compact model for information analysis. Processing of information is fully described by Bayesian probability revision. And this provides enough structure to rigorously specify a cost and value of information expression and to provide a general theorem on value across all decision problems defined on a particular set of states.

In turn, complications arise if we admit to costly analysis or separation between the user and the producer of the information. With costly analysis we regard the expected utility measurement as being too costly to specify. While realistic this unfortunately draws us away from the strict Bayesian revision description of information processing. With producer-user separation we actually have a game in the sense that the evaluator's outcome depends on a personal choice as well as the choice of another individual. We originally studied this setting by relying on exogenous specification of the decision maker's behavior; and subsequently we looked at a more restrictive setting, the principal-agent model, in order to demonstrate an analysis that simultaneously specifies both individuals' choice behavior. It is important to remember, though, that description via global utility measurement is impossible here (provided we accept the outlined assessment conditions) simply because such a measure does not in general exist.

A remaining question, or set of questions, in the study of economic aspects of information concerns the importance of markets. We might, in fact, inquire into the idea of purchasing information in a market (as when we go to the bookstore or auto diagnostic clinic); or we might view the decision maker's acts as representing alternative trades in an organized market (such as buying and selling securities). We conclude our study of information analysis by briefly commenting on the importance of these markets.

INFORMATION MARKETS

Rather than structure our analysis around the abstract idea of selecting one system η from an available set H we might envision an organized information market. Consider acquiring various wine encyclopedia and pamphlets at your local bookstore, or searching the management consulting market. From here we might even indulge in the economist's dream and construct a demand curve, plotting quantity of information demanded against price per unit.[1]

This is, in fact, a fairly natural exercise because information is, recall, a factor of production. It is used in producing quality decisions. Hence its demand is a derived demand. (Indeed our study would be vastly different if we admitted to direct consumption aspects of information, such as enjoyment from reading annual reports or budgets.) And economists readily deal with the (derived) demand for factors of production. Of course, we must have an explicitly uncertain production setting; otherwise the demand will be nil at any positive price. And we must also be careful in specifying what we mean by "quantity of information." Here the subpartitioning idea in Theorem 3 can be readily exploited.

The major difficulty here concerns property rights. Use of an ordinary factor of production such as labor or fuel oil "destroys ' the factor in the sense that once used it is no longer available for another productive endeavor. But information can be quite a different story. Has reading destroyed this book? Is the management consultant's advice inapplicable anywhere else in the industry? Does studying a wine tasting report prior to selecting the evening's wine destroy the taster's report so that a friend cannot use it? Unless property rights can be strictly enforced (this book is "protected" by a copyright) to prevent resale or the information has strictly private use (such as might be the case with a medical check up to detect deficiencies in your diet), information markets are quite distinct from the idealizations of classical economic theory. And in the extreme, public good aspects are involved as when the government produces and publishes agricultural crop statistics, fuel consumption estimates, and a census. Information, then, takes on atypical characteristics when compared with a more conventional factor of production in a (factor) market setting.[2]

MARKET ACTS

A similar picture emerges if we interpret the decision maker's acts as trades in a set of organized markets. If the markets are perfect so that one individual's acts do not affect the price, and if we are examining information that is private to our individual, no difficulties emerge. But consider a wine or financial securities market. Both items are of uncertain quality and we could envision information being made available to all participants. Prices would then be expected to change. Indeed, we have a large literature documenting security price changes associated with the release of annual reports.[3] But with price changes we also must begin to consider wealth effects. If you hold a particular security and if public information of a distressing nature is released, its relative price will (presumably) decline, as will your wealth. So the setting is more subtle than simply improving the quality of act selection. The information, by changing wealth, can also change the available acts.[4] (Return to Theorem 3 and carefully note that this was assumed away in that setting.)

An intermediate setting is even more fascinating. Suppose enough individuals acquire and trade on private information so that prices change. Those without the information may now be able to infer at least some of that information from the prices. Does the price of wine, for example, in some sense reflect its quality? This is, in fact, the notion of market (informational) efficiency.[5]

We have, in other words, provided the building blocks for a continued study of information. But we have by no means exhausted that study.[6] There is much more to be discovered and said about the economic aspects of information.

FOOTNOTES

1. This has been done by Kihlstrom (1974, 1974a).
2. See Hirshleifer (1973), Hirshleifer and Riley (1979), Demski and Feltham (1976), especially Chapter 8, and Beaver (1977) for additional discussion.
3. See Foster (1978).
4. Fama and Laffer (1971) and Hirshleifer (1971) initiated a long study of this phenomenon. Its application to financial reporting is discussed in Demski and Feltham (1976), Beaver (1977), Ng (1977), Hakansson et al. (1979), and Ohlson and Buckman (1980).
5. Beaver (1977) provides a recent review. Also see Grossman and Stiglitz (1976). Moreover, this interest in prices that somehow reflect information available to actors in the market raises questions of how the prices are actually formed. It is possible to show, for example, that the winning bid in an auction where everyone has private information about the item being auctioned actually converges, with many bidders, to the item's value given all of the information available. See Wilson (1977) and Milgrom (1979).
6. For example, we might now focus on regulation of information production and the political aspects thereof, as in Watts (1977) and Watts and Zimmerman (1978).

BIBLIOGRAPHY

Abdel-Magid, M. F., "Toward a Better Understanding of the Role of Measurement in Accounting," *Accounting Review* (April, 1979).

Ackoff, R. L., *Scientific Method: Optimizing Applied Research Decisions* (New York: Wiley, 1962).

Ackoff, R. L., "Management Misinformation Systems," *Management Science* (December, 1967).

American Accounting Association, *A Statement of Basic Accounting Theory* (1966).

Anscombe, F. J., and R. J. Aumann, "A Definition of Subjective Probability," *Annals of Math. Stat.* (1963).

Arrow, K. J., *Social Choice and Individual Values* (New York: Wiley, 1963).

Avriel, M. and A. C. Williams, "The Value of Information and Stochastic Programming," *Operations Research* (Sept.–Oct., 1970).

Baiman, S., "The Evaluation and Choice of Internal Information Systems within a Multiperson World," *Journal of Accounting Research* (Spring, 1975).

Baumol, W. J., and R. C. Bushnell, "Error Produced by Linearization in Mathematical Programming," *Econometrica* (July, 1967).

Beaver, W. H., "The Nature of Mandated Disclosure," in *Report of the SEC Advisory Committee on Corporate Disclosure* (U.S. Govt. Printing Office, 1977).

Beaver, W. H., and J. S. Demski, "The Nature of Income Measurement," *Accounting Review* (January, 1979).

Buffa, E. S., and J. G. Miller, *Production-Inventory Systems: Planning and Control* (Homewood, Ill.: Irwin, 1979).

Chambers, R. J., "Measurement in Accounting," *Journal of Accounting Research* (Spring, 1965).

Chase, R. B., and N. S. Aquilano, *Production and Operations Management* (Homewood, Ill.: Irwin, 1977).

Coombs, C. H., et al., *Mathematical Psychology: An Elementary Introduction* (Englewood Cliffs, N.J.: Prentice-Hall, 1970).

Demski, J. S., "An Accounting System Structured on a Linear Programming Model," *Accounting Review* (October 1967).

Demski, J. S., "Some Considerations in Sensitizing an Optimization Model," *J. Ind. Eng.* (September, 1968).

Demski, J. S., "Information Improvement Bounds," *Journal of Accounting Research* (Spring, 1972).

Demski, J. S., "Rational Choice of Accounting Method for a Class of Partnerships," *Journal of Accounting Research* (Autumn, 1973).

Demski, J. S., "The General Impossibility of Normative Accounting Standards," *Accounting Review* (October, 1973a).

Demski, J. S., "An Economic Analysis of the Chambers' Normative Standard," *Accounting Review* (July, 1976).

Demski, J. S., "A Simple Case of Indeterminate Financial Reporting," *Accounting Journal* (forthcoming, 1980).

Demski, J. S., and G. A. Feltham, "Forecast Evaluation," *Accounting Review* (July, 1972).

Demski, J. S., and G. A. Feltham, *Cost Determination: A Conceptual Approach* (Ames, Iowa: Iowa State University Press, 1976).

Demski, J. S., and G. A. Feltham, "Economic Incentives in Budgetary Control Systems," *Accounting Review* (April, 1978).

Dillon, R. D., and J. F. Nash, "The True Relevance of Relevant Costs," *Accounting Review* (January, 1978).

Dittman, D. and P. Prakash, "Cost Variance Investigation: Markovian Control Versus Optimal Control," *Accounting Review* (April, 1979).

Dopuch, N., et al., *Cost Accounting: Accounting Data for Management's Decisions* (New York: Harcourt, forthcoming, 1981).

Earl, B., *Groups and Fields* (New York: McGraw Hill, 1963).

Eilon, S., "Mathematical Modeling for Management," *Interfaces* (February, 1974).

Eilon, S., "Five Approaches to Aggregate Production Planning," *AIIE Transactions* (June, 1975).

Fama, E. F., and A. B. Laffer, "Information and Capital Markets," *Journal of Business* (July, 1971).

Fama, E. F., and M. H. Miller, *The Theory of Finance* (New York: Holt, Rinehart and Winston, 1972).

Feltham, G. A., *Information Evaluation, SAR#5* (American Accounting Association, 1972).

Feltham, G. A., "Cost Aggregation: An Information Economics Analysis," *Journal of Accounting Research* (Spring, 1977).

Fishburn, P. C., *Utility Theory for Decision Making* (New York: Wiley, 1970).

Fishburn, P. C., *Mathematics of Decision Theory* (UNESCO, 1972).

Foster, G., *Financial Statement Analysis* (Englewood Cliffs, N.J.: Prentice-Hall, 1978).

Gould, J. P., "Risk, Stochastic Preference, and the Value of Information," *Journal of Economic Theory* (May, 1974).

Green, J. R., and J. Laffont, *Incentives in Public Decision Making* (Amsterdam, Holland: North-Holland, 1979).

Grossman, S. J., and J. E. Stiglitz, "Information and Competitive Price Systems," *American Economic Review* (May, 1976).

Grossman, S. J., et al., "A Bayesian Approach to the Production of Information and Learning by Doing," *Review of Economic Studies* (October, 1977).

Hakansson, N. et. al., "Sufficient and Necessary Conditions for Information to Have Social Value in Pure Exchange," unpublished, U. of California at Berkeley (1979).

Harris, M. and A. Raviv, "Some Results on Incentive Contracts with Applications to Education and Employment, Health Insurance, and Law Enforcement," *American Economic Review* (March, 1978).

Harrison, J. M., "Independence and Calibration in Decision Analysis," *Management Science* (November, 1977).

Hertz, D. B., "Risk Analysis in Capital Investment," *Harvard Business Review* (Jan.–Feb., 1964).

Hilton, R. W., "The Determinants of Cost Information Value: An Illustrative Analysis," *Journal of Accounting Research* (Autumn, 1979).

Hilton, R. W., "The Determinants of Information Value: Synthesizing some General Results," unpublished, Cornell University (1979a).

Hirshleifer, J., *Investment, Interest, and Capital* (Englewood Cliffs, N.J.: Prentice-Hall, 1970).

Hirshleifer, J., "The Private and Social Value of Information and the Reward to Inventive Activity," *American Economic Review* (September, 1971).

Hirshleifer, J., "Where Are We in the Theory of Information?" *American Economic Review* (May, 1973).

Hirshleifer, J. and J. G. Riley, "The Analytics of Uncertainty and Information—An Expository Survey," *Journal of Economic Literature* (December, 1979).

Holloway, C. A., *Decision Making Under Uncertainty* (Englewood Cliffs, N.J.: Prentice-Hall, 1979).

Holloway, C. A., et al., "Comparison of a Multi-Pass Heuristic Decomposition Procedure with Other Resource-Constrained Project Scheduling Procedures," *Management Science* (September, 1979).

Holmstrom, B., "Moral Hazard and Observability," *Bell Journal of Economics* (Spring, 1979).

Holt, C. L., et al., *Planning Production, Inventories, and Work Force* (Englewood Cliffs, N.J.: Prentice Hall, 1960).

Horngren, C. T., *Cost Accounting: A Managerial Emphasis* (Englewood Cliffs, N.J.: Prentice-Hall, 1977).

Howard, R. A., "The Foundations of Decision Analysis," *IEEE Trans. On Systems Science and Cybernetics* (September, 1968).

Howard, R. A., "Proximal Decision Analysis," *Management Science* (May, 1971).

Huang, C., et al., "Sharp Bounds on the Value of Perfect Information," *Operations Research* (Jan.–Feb., 1977).

Ijiri, Y., *Management Goals and Accounting for Control* (Chicago: Rand McNally, 1965).

Ijiri, Y., *Theory of Accounting Measurement, SAR#10* (American Accounting Association, 1976).

Itami, H., *Adaptive Behavior: Management Control and Information Analysis, SAR#15* (American Accounting Association, 1977).

Jensen, M. C., and W. H. Meckling, "Theory of the Firm: Managerial Behavior, Agency Costs and Ownership Structure," *Journal of Financial Economics* (October, 1976).

Kaplan, R. S., "The Significance and Investigation of Cost Variances: Survey and Extensions," *Journal of Accounting Research* (Autumn, 1975).

Kassouf, S., *Normative Decision Making* (Englewood Cliffs, N.J.: Prentice-Hall, 1970).

Keen, P. G., and M. S. Scott-Morton, *Decision Support Systems* (Reading, Mass.: Addison-Wesley, 1978).

Kelly, J. S., *Arrow Impossibility Theorems* (New York: Academic Press, 1978).

Kihlstrom, R., "A Bayesian Model of Demand for Information about Product Quality," *International Economic Review* (February, 1974).

Kihlstrom, R., "A General Theory of Demand for Information about Product Quality," *Journal of Economic Theory* (August, 1974a).

Krantz, D. H., et al., *Foundations of Measurement* (New York: Academic Press, 1971).

Kreps, D. M., "A Representation Theorem for 'Preference for Flexibility,' " *Econometrica* (May, 1979).

Kreps, D. M., and E. L. Porteus, "Temporal von Neumann-Morgenstern and Induced Preferences," *Journal of Economic Theory* (Feb., 1979).

Kwon, Y. K., et al., "Stochastic Dominance and Information Value," *Journal of Economic Theory* (April, 1979).

Laffont, J., "Risk, Stochastic Preference, and the Value of Information: A Comment," *Journal of Economic Theory* (June, 1976).

LaValle, I., "On Cash Equivalents and Information Evaluation in Decisions Under Uncertainty," Parts I, II, and III, *J. of Amer. Statistical Association* (March, 1968).

Lee, W. B., and B. M. Khumawala, "Simulation Testing of Aggregate Production Planning Models in an Implementation Methodology," *Management Science* (February, 1974).

Libby, R. and P. C. Fishburn, "Behavioral Models of Risk Taking in Business Decisions: A Survey and Evaluation," *Journal of Accounting Research* (Autumn, 1977).

Luce, R. D., and H. Raiffa, *Games and Decisions* (New York: Wiley, 1957).

Magee, R. P., "A Simulation Analysis of Alternative Cost Variance Investigation Models," *Accounting Review* (July, 1976).

Marschak, J., "The Payoff-Relevant Description of States and Acts," *Econometrica* (October, 1963).

Marschak, J., "Economics of Information Systems," *J. of Amer. Statistical Association* (March, 1971).

Marschak, J. and K. Miyasawa, "Economic Comparability of Information Systems," *International Economic Review* (June, 1968).

Marschak, J. and R. Radner, *Economic Theory of Teams* (New Haven, Conn.: Yale University Press, 1972).

Marshall, R., "Determining an Optimal Accounting Information System for an Unidentified User," *Journal of Accounting Research* (Autumn, 1972).

McGuire, C. B., "Comparisons of Information Structures," in McGuire and Radner (1972).

McGuire, C. B., and R. Radner (eds.), *Decision and Organization* (Amsterdam, Holland: North Holland, 1972).

Merkhofer, M. W., "The Value of Information Given Decision Flexibility," *Management Science* (March, 1977).

Milgrom, P. R., "A Convergence Theorem for Competitive Bidding with Differential Information," *Econometrica* (May, 1979).

Mirrlees, J. A., "Notes on Welfare Economics, Information and Uncertainty," in Balch et al. (eds.), *Essays on Economic Behavior Under Uncertainty* (Amsterdam, Holland: North-Holland, 1974).

Mirrlees, J. A., "The Optimal Structure of Incentives and Authority within an Organization," *Bell Journal of Economics* (Spring, 1976).

Mock, T. J., *Measurement and Accounting Information Criteria, SAR#13* (American Accounting Association, 1976).

Mock, T. J., and M. A. Vasarhelyi, "A Synthesis of the Information Economics and Lens Models," *Journal of Accounting Research* (Autumn, 1978).

Morris, W. T., "On the Art of Modeling," *Management Science* (August, 1967).

Mossin, J., *The Economic Efficiency of Financial Markets* (Lexington, Mass.: Lexington, 1977).

Nelson, R. T., et al., "Centralized Scheduling and Priority Implementation Heuristics for a Dynamic Job Shop Model," *AIIE Transactions* (March, 1977).

Ng, D. S., Pareto-Optimality of Authentic Information," *Journal of Finance* (December, 1977).

Ohlson, J. C., "The Complete Ordering of Information Alternatives for a Class of Portfolio Selection Models," *Journal of Accounting Research* (Autumn, 1975).

Ohlson, J. A., and A. G. Buckman, "Toward a Theory of Financial Accounting," *Journal of Finance* (May, 1980).

Parzen, E., *Modern Probability Theory and Its Applications* (New York: Wiley, 1960).

Patell, J. M., "The API and the Design of Experiments," *Journal of Accounting Research* (Autumn, 1979).

Ponssard, J. P., "A Note on Information Value Theory for Experiments Defined in Extensive Form," *Management Science* (December, 1975).

Ponssard, J. P., "On the Concept of the Value of Information in Competitive Situations," *Management Science* (March, 1976).

Ponssard, J. and S. Zamir, "Zero-Sum Sequential Games with Incomplete Information," *International J. of Game Theory* (1973).

Pratt, J. W., "Risk Aversion in the Small and in the Large," *Econometrica* (January, 1964).

Radner, R., "Normative Theory of Individual Decision: An Introduction," in McGuire and Radner (1972).

Raiffa, H., *Decision Analysis: Introductory Lectures on Choices Under Uncertainty* (Reading, Mass.: Addison-Wesley, 1968).

Raiffa, H. and R. Schlaifer, *Applied Statistical Decision Theory* (Cambridge, Mass.: MIT Press, 1968).

Ross, S., "The Economic Theory of Agency: The Principal's Problem," *American Economic Review* (May, 1973).

Ross, S., "On the Economic Theory of Agency and the Principle of Similarity," in Balch et al. (eds.), *Essays on Economic Behavior Under Uncertainty* (Amsterdam, Holland: North-Holland, 1974).

Savage, L. J., *The Foundations of Statistics* (New York: Wiley, 1954).

Schlaifer, R., *Analysis of Decisions Under Uncertainty* (New York: McGraw-Hill, 1969).

Sen, A. K., *Collective Choice and Social Welfare* (San Francisco, Ca.: Holden-Day, 1970).

Shavell, S., "Risk Sharing and Incentives in the Principal and Agent Relationship," *Bell Journal of Economics* (Spring, 1979).

Simon, H. A., "Theories of Bounded Rationality," in McGuire and Radner (1972).

Smallwood, R. D., "A Decision Analysis of Model Selection," *IEEE Trans. On Systems Science and Cybernetics* (September, 1968).

Spence, M. and R. Zeckhauser, "Insurance, Information, and Individual Action," *American Economic Review* (May, 1971).

Sterling, R. R., *Theory of the Measurement of Enterprise Income* (Lawrence, Kans.: University Press of Kansas, 1970).

Stiglitz, J. E., "Risk Sharing and Incentives in Sharecropping," *Review of Economic Studies* (April, 1974).

Sundem, G. L., "A Game Theory Model of the Information Evaluator and the Decision Maker," *Journal of Accounting Research* (Spring, 1979).

Suppes, P., *Axiomatic Set Theory* (New York: Dover, 1972).

U.S. General Accounting Office, *Guidelines for Model Evaluation, PAD-79-17* (January, 1979).

von Neumann, J. and O. Morgenstern, *Theory of Games and Economic Behavior* (Princeton, N.J.: Princeton University Press, 1947).

Wagner, H. M., *Principles of Operations Research* (Englewood Cliffs, N.J.: Prentice-Hall, 1975).

Warren, C. S., "Confirmation Informativeness," *Journal of Accounting Research* (Spring, 1974).

Watts, R. L., "Corporate Financial Statements, A Product of the Market and Political Processes," *Australian Journal of Management* (April, 1977).

Watts, R. L., and J. L. Zimmerman, "Towards a Positive Theory of the Determination of Accounting Standards," *Accounting Review* (January, 1978).

Wilson, R. B., "On the Theory of Syndicates," *Econometrica* (January, 1968).

Wilson, R. B., "The Structure of Incentives for Decentralization under Uncertainty," in Guilbaud (ed.), *La Decision* (Center National de la Recherche Scientifique, 1969).

Wilson, R. B., "Informational Economies of Scale," *Bell Journal of Economics* (Spring, 1975).

Wilson, R. B., "A Bidding Model of Perfect Competition," *Review of Economic Studies* (1977).

INDEX